PREF

D1589410

by
Erika Munk

I like to consider this happy event a sign that the 80s—at least the theatrical and theater-critical 80s, which are as benighted as all other aspects of this time in this place—are really coming to an end. Who would have thought two or three years ago that anyone would be interested in publishing, or for that matter reading, a work so totally alien to the ever-more-formalist evolution of contemporary criticism and the ever-more-consumerist nature of contemporary arts journalism? Goldman seems quite daft: she judges playwrights on the grounds of their relative humanity, and plays on their social truths. As we read her heroic, uplifting, sentimental summaries of works both famous and forgotten, she can also seem a little simple-minded: is this all there is to say about Chekhov, or the most important thing? Does writing in the same tone of voice about Chekhov and T. G. Murray leave us any wiser? Isn't she committing as merciless a reduction as does the most obsessed deconstructionist?

Yes—but her very flaws can help us redress the terrible imbalance of our criticism. There's no danger of Goldmanism taking over either our scholarly journals or our weekly tipsheets; what she can do is make us see that we don't have to think it naive to write about a play's subject, embarrassing to assume its point of view has real-life analogues, and completely humiliating to judge it by its social ethics. The heart of her argument is her introduction's impassioned statement that theater is both a mirror and a force for change; while too many revolutions have gone under history's bridge (and down the drain) since Goldman wrote this book for us to find the question of "becoming part of the process or [being] left behind" one whose answer is unambiguous, absenting ourselves totally from "the process" has left both playwright and audience powerless, peripheral.

Emma Goldman's anarchism freed her to take art seriously in a way that Marxist leftwingers couldn't, wedded as they then were to the idea of a cultural superstructure determined by an economic base. As she wrote in *Living My Life,* "One very popular playwright expressed surprise that such an arch-destructionist as I should care for creative drama. I tried to explain to him that anarchism represented the urge of expression in every phase of life and art. Seeing his uncomprehending look, I remarked: 'Even those who only *think* they are dramatists will have opportunity in a free society. If they lack real talent, they will still have other honourable professions to choose from, like shoe-making, for instance.'" (I wonder whether the poor playwright stuck to his last in the face of her putdown?) True to her conviction that all urges toward expression should be honored, Goldman mixed political and cultural enterprise as she agitated throughout America, and though her taste was surprisingly more conformist than her ideology, she has much to teach about integrating our intellectual lives, about demanding bread and roses too. It's also healthily humbling to see how alive some of the subjects central to even the second-rate playwrights she mentions still are today: abortion, sexual plagues, the ravages of piousness.

As for her horrid adrenalin-raising chapter on Strindberg, which no feminist could leave unmentioned, I'll kindly attribute it to the fact that the work on this book paralleled the time of her greatest difficulties with her lover Ben Reitman, who was unfaithful, a physical coward (most unlike her), and, more to the point, obsessed with his mother. "No man I had loved had ever so paralyzed my will before." Just as Goldman's politics led her to write about Gorky and Yeats as though they were embarked on the same project, her private life urged her to embrace Strindberg, whose grim misanthropy seems in such contradiction to her spirit.

Emma Goldman's theater writing was impelled by her ideology, by her private life, by everything except a disinterested concern for the structures of dramaturgy. And precisely because of this, it can tell us something that is still, more than ever, worth hearing: that theater is urgent and connected.

INTRODUCTION

by
Harry G. Carlson

Emma Goldman's unpretentious 1914 survey of modern drama may seem an unlikely candidate for reconsideration in the late 1980's. She was an anarchist, wasn't she, not an authority on drama? Where most professional critics of the day were busy attempting to chart the shifting winds of style from realism to anti-realism and back again, she was unconcerned about the technique of drama. What mattered were the vital social themes that made the plays come alive, and her lively and provocative discussions of these themes make her a delight to read.

Despite her amateur status as drama expert, Goldman had more than a casual connection with the arts in general and the theatre in particular. One might say that her political and theatrical interests were closely related, a not uncommon phenomenon in the history of either politics or the theatre. A theatrical flair and a fine appreciation of the high drama of history made her a dynamic polemical lecturer and political activist in the decades flanking the turn of the century.

Born the daughter of the manager of a subsidized theatre in Kovno, Lithuania, in 1869, Goldman emigrated to the United States in her late teens. A theatrical group with which she worked at the turn of the century, The Progressive Stage Society, helped to spearhead the experimental little theatre movement. In 1905 and 1906 she managed the American tour of the Russian-speaking Paul Orleneff troupe, which included the great actress Alla Nazimova, who startled S. N. Behrman years later with "her calm declaration that she would like to do a play about Emma Goldman and play the part of Emma."[1] Despite the language barrier, Orleneff performances attracted admiring audiences and brought Goldman in contact with theatre people like Ethel and John Barrymore, Grace George, Minnie Maddern Fiske, and Arthur Hornblow, editor of the important *Theatre Magazine*.[2] A decade later her friends included members of the important Provincetown Players—Susan Glaspell, John Reed, and Louise Bryant (a period dramatized in part in Warren Beatty's film about Reed, *Reds,* in which the role of Emma Goldman was played by Maureen Stapleton).

The Social Significance of Modern Drama grew out of a six-week lecture series at New York's Berkeley Theatre in 1914, but would never have appeared if an adoring young member of the audience, Paul Munter, a stenographer, had not taken notes and presented Goldman with a typescript. Her rapport with audiences so impressed a representative of Oscar Hammerstein that he offered her a vaudeville stint at the Victoria Theatre. She describes in her autobiography, *Living My Life,*[3] how, although amused, she was intrigued, and accepted an invitation to visit the theatre.

The manager informed me that he would have to try me out first, to see what was the drawing power of my name. We went back-stage, where he introduced me to some of the performers. It was a motley crowd of dancers, acrobats, and men with trained dogs. "I'll have to sandwich you in," the manager said. He was not sure whether I was to come on before the high kicker or after the trained dogs.

Wisely realizing that her ideas would be out of place in such a context, she fled, in the process learning a lesson that can serve as a key to understanding the vital role she played in the letters and politics of her time: she never permitted anyone to "sandwich" her in anywhere, whether as a critic of drama or of society. To understand her attitude toward criticism, it is necessary to understand that though her view of life was comprehensively political, she was never as narrowly ideological or ruthlessly fanatical as she was portrayed in the press. Emma Goldman was herself—an idealist often vague about specific goals, sometimes childishly naïve, but always a rock-solid figure of courage and integrity, bringing to bear her own anarchist brand of social compassion in the service of whatever interest or cause that attracted her attention at the moment.

The New York lectures on drama were not an isolated chapter in her life. In 1897 she had journeyed down into a Welsh coal mine to lecture on George Bernard Shaw. A decade later in the United States she brought the word about the general ferment of ideas in contemporary European drama to rapt audiences across the country, no small accomplishment, given the conservative temper of the times. Rebecca West was probably too generous in crediting her with making Shaw's ideas popular on this side of the Atlantic, but Goldman's impact was considerable. Henry Miller was inspired enough by her book to hurry off to New York to explore experimental theatres. He said she "opened up the whole world of European culture for me and gave a new impetus to my life, as well as direction."[4] She preached that Ibsen,

Strindberg, Hauptmann, Tolstoy, Shaw, and Galsworthy were "the social iconoclasts of our time. They know that . . . man must throw off the dead weight of the past, with all its ghosts and spooks, if he is to go foot free to meet the future. This is the social significance which differentiates modern dramatic art from art for art's sake."

Goldman found plenty of social causes to defend in a career that began with her radicalization in 1887 and ended with her death in Canada in 1940, in political exile. Along the way there were many arrests, several jail terms, and her deportation to Russia as an enemy of the state in 1919. The radicalization came about after the Haymarket tragedy in Chicago, where a group of anarchists were charged in a bomb-throwing incident and executed after a trial that even at the time was recognized as unjust. In 1892 she was involved in, though not arrested for, an unsuccessful assassination attempt on Henry Clay Frick, a steel magnate. When Frick's ruthless efforts to crush a labor union resulted in the deaths of some workers, Goldman and her longtime friend and associate Alexander Berkman decided that the time was ripe for an *Attentat.* Berkman was captured after shooting Frick in his office and served a ten-year prison sentence.

In 1901 came the event that made her the most notorious woman in America. A banner headline told the whole story: "ASSASSIN OF PRESIDENT McKINLEY AN ANARCHIST. CONFESSES TO HAVING BEEN INCITED BY EMMA GOLDMAN. WOMAN ANARCHIST WANTED." Though totally innocent—the "confession" was a fabrication—she was arrested in Chicago and held for a time while the police in Buffalo, where the assassination took place, tried to have her extradited. Typically, she reacted directly contrary to her own best interests. While her fellow anarchists wanted her to repudiate the murderer, Leon Czolgosz, she thought the man belonged in a mental institution, not a prison, and openly expressed sympathy for his plight. She was finally released for lack of evidence, but in the eyes of many she was guilty.

Over the next decade Goldman's notoriety increased, but so did her popularity. Her lectures (when she wasn't prevented by court orders from giving them) were inspiring to a generation who felt stifled by conventional attitudes on a wide range of social issues from art to politics to sex. It is some measure of the furor she was capable of arousing that many of the issues she championed are still regarded provocative and controversial today: free love, birth control, and a sympathetic public understanding of homosexuality. Her stubborn battles to gain hearings for "progressive ideas" of all kinds, no matter how unpopular, led to the founding of the American Civil Liberties. But of course her favorite cause was anarchism, which she defined as "the philosophy of a new social order based on liberty unrestricted by man-made law; the theory that all forms of government rest on violence, and are therefore wrong and harmful, as well as unnecessary." Her favorite targets were capitalism, the state, institutionalized religion, and private property, and her favorite solution for the social problems that she blamed on these vested interests was revolutionary anarchism.

Given her radical ideas on sex and politics, it is not difficult to understand how she could incur hostility from the right, but she was equally adept at alienating the left. Political expedience was simply not in her vocabulary. She describes in her autobiography addressing a group of feminists who

could not excuse my critical attitude towards the bombastic and impossible claims of the suffragists as to the wonderful things they would do when they got political power. They branded me as an enemy of woman's freedom, and . . . denounced me.

The incident reminded me of a similar occasion when I had lectured on woman's inhumanity to man. Always on the side of the underdog, I resented my sex's placing every evil at the door of the male. . . . The inconsistencies of my sex keep the poor male dangling between the idol and the brute, the darling and the beast, the helpless child and the conqueror of worlds. . . . When [the female] has learned to be as self-centred and as determined as [the male] is, when she gains the courage to delve into life as he does and pay the price for it, she will achieve her liberation, and incidentally also help him become free. Whereupon my women hearers would rise up against me and cry: "You're a man's woman and not one of us."

Like Ibsen (one of her favorites), her goal was not female liberation, but human liberation.

Goldman's deportation to Russia in 1919 made her a martyr in many circles. Two years later, however, when she became disillusioned and voiced her opposition to the Bolsheviks, many of the same intellectuals who supported her earlier—not only radicals, but liberals like Bertrand Russell—found her an embarrassment. What she singled out as fundamental flaws and injustices in Soviet communism, they excused or blinked at as the temporary shortcomings inevitable in any new social system.

"Red Emma," the dangerous bomb-thrower and moral leper that threatened the youth of America, was a fiction created by the hysteria of a period when Americans feared that labor unions and other trouble-making forces would turn the country communist, a hysteria that would return again thirty years later. However much she disapproved of the economic evils of capitalism, the primary enemy for her was any kind of centralized government that attempted to oppress the human spirit, to deprive the individual of his or her inherent dignity and worth.

"Revolution" and "revolutionary" were important words for her, and they occur often in *Social Significance*. But as she uses them, they are different from the catchwords that usually define the most important political phenomenon of modern times. She described the difference in the Afterword of her 1922 book on Russia.

[T]he great mission of revolution, of the **Social Revolution**, is a **fundamental transvaluation of values.** A transvaluation not only of social, but also of human values. . . . The sense of justice and equality, the love of liberty and of human brotherhood—these fundamentals of the real regeneration of society—the Communist State suppressed to the point of extermination. Man's instinctive sense of equity was branded as weak sentimentality; human dignity and liberty became a bourgeois superstition; the sanctity of life, which is the very essence of social reconstruction, was condemned as un-revolutionary, almost counter-revolutionary. . . . This perversion of . . . ethical values soon crystallized into the all-dominating slogan of the Communist Party: **The end Justifies all means.**

Goldman's broadly humanist definition of "revolutionary" helps to explain some of the apparently quirky surprises in her book, such as in her separate discussions of Strindberg and Yeats. Even today, a common critical approach to Strindberg's *The Father* is to treat the play as little more than an autobiographical document, the highly subjective product of a madman's fevered brain. In contrast, she saw Strindberg consciously evoking an important—and radical—psycho-social theme.

Motherhood, much praised, poetized, and hailed as a wonderful thing, is in reality very often the greatest deterrent influence in the life of the child. . . . [The mother] binds the child to herself with a thousand threads which never grant sufficient freedom for mental and spiritual expansion. . . . The mother enslaves with kindness,—a bondage harder to bear and more difficult to escape than the brutal fist of the father. . . . In portraying motherhood, as it really is, August Strindberg is conveying a vital and revolutionary message . . .

And who else could think Yeats—whom Goldman admits was suspicious of plays with social themes—capable of writing, in *Where There is Nothing*, "as true an interpretation of the philosophy of Anarchism as could be given by its best exponents"?[5] Behind the story of a man who rejects the forces in society that would inhibit his instinct toward self-realization she senses the same utopian dream that enervated her own faith in anarchism.

Paul Ruttledge: The Laws were the first sin. They were the first mouthful of the apple; the moment man had made them he began to die; we must put out the Laws as I put out this candle . . . [Men] began to build big houses and big towns. They grew wealthy. . . . We must put out the towns as I put out this candle. But that is not all, for man created a worse thing. . . . Man built up the Church. We must destroy the Church, we must put it out as I put out this candle. . . . We must destroy everything that has Law and Number.

For Goldman, the revolutionary significance of Yeats's play was in the message it carried "of the destruction of every institution—State, Property, and Church—that enslaves humanity. **For where there is nothing, there man begins.**"

There are other surprises as well in *Social Significance*. The theme in Hermann Sudermann's *Magda* is defended in terms as controversial today as when they were stated: "the question of woman's right to motherhood with or without the sanction of State and Church." The discussions of Stanley Houghton's *Hindle Wakes* and Githa Sowerby's *Rutherford and Son* focus deserved attention on forgotten plays that herald feminist themes of the 1970's and '80s. And the sensitive handling of the socio-sexual themes in Wedekind's vital *Spring's Awakening* is a half-century ahead of its time. "The critics," she argues,

could see naught in Wedekind, except a base, perverted, almost diabolic nature bereft of all finer feeling. But professional critics seldom see below the surface; else they would discover beneath the grin and satire of Frank Wedekind a sensitive soul, deeply stirred by the heart-rending tragedies about him.

Most surprising, perhaps, is that Maeterlinck and Rostand are praised for their revolutionary sentiments. The personal note is evident here too; Goldman, like Chantecler in Rostand's play, was a victim of the mob spirit, whether on top or at the bottom, using the most cruel and contemptible methods to drag the idealist down; to revile and persecute him—aye, even to kill him—for the unpardonable sin of proclaiming the ideal. They cannot forgive Chantecler for worshiping the sun. . . . It is vital to understand that . . . though we cannot wake the dawn, we must prepare the people to greet the rising sun.

Goldman is never more fervent than when writing about Ibsen and Hauptmann. The social evils evoked in Ibsen's plays were the very ones she saw as most dangerous: "the Social Lie and the paralyzing effect of Duty, . . . the uselessness and evil of Sacrifice, the dreary Lack of Joy and of Purpose in Work, . . . [the] most pernicious and destructive elements in life." And she undoubtedly found it easy to identify with the protagonist in *Enemy of the People:* a rebel who is ostracized when he speaks the truth about social corruption. But Hauptmann, for her, is more human, more universal: "never as aloof as the iconoclast Ibsen, never as bitter as the soul dissector Strindberg, nor yet as set as the crusader Tolstoy." His play *Lonely Lives* contains "the lesson that the real revolutionist,—the dreamer, the creative artist, the iconoclast in whatever line,—is fated to be misunderstood, not only by his own kin, but often by his own comrades."

Although Goldman saw drama as a weapon for raising political awareness, she recognized that art has truths to tell that cannot be reduced to slogans or calls for political action. And so she is as critical of the "average radical," who "is as hidebound by mere terms as the man devoid of all ideas," as she is of the conservative who "sees danger only in the advocacy of the Red Flag." Both "have to learn that any mode of creative work, which with true perception portrays social wrongs earnestly and boldly, may be a . . . a more powerful inspiration than the wildest harangue of the soapbox orator." Even Shaw, one of her idols, comes under fire when she feels he sacrifices art for ideology.

As the propagandist Shaw is limited, dogmatic, and set. Indeed, the most zealous Puritan could not be more antagonistic to social theories differing from his own. But the artist, if he is sincere at all, must go to life as the source of his inspiration, and life is beyond dogmas . . .

Thanks to Goldman's inherent fairmindedness, her sure instincts for the social dynamics of drama, the importance and continuing relevance of her book is as a modest but eloquent contribution to a critical debate that began in earnest in the last quarter of the nineteenth century. It was then that critics like George Brandes proclaimed a new responsibility for literature, in the process profoundly influencing Ibsen, Strindberg, and later Goldman (who admired him for writing understandingly about Russian anarchist Peter Kropotkin). Brandes called for literature that would "debate the issues of the day." A century later the demand was that literature be "socially relevant." In each instance there was a political subtext. Brandes favored themes that would advance the liberalism that he saw as chief legacy of the French Revolution. "Social relevance" meant, and still means, more often than not, addressing themes that are faithful to a Marxist agenda.

Goldman, in contrast, is a tireless humanist. Instead of social relevance in art, she preached what would best be described in the 1980s as a process of "consciousness-raising." Drama had an important role to play in this process, and she appreciated that the role could be played in different ways—provided it was done seriously. The only aesthetic principle of which she disapproved—indeed, even heaped scorn upon—was "art for art's sake." Art was too important, life was too important, for trivial games. For all her anti-religious pronouncements, the goal she set for herself was sacred (a rabbi once described her as a very religious person). It was a society of enlightened, free individuals, unbound by unjust social, political, or moral restrictions or prejudices. To the extent that she believed the goal was possible, she was an incurable optimist, steadfastly advancing the banner of anarchism long after the cause had ceased to play an influential role in politics, either in Europe or America. But she was also sympathetic to artists that were labelled—and still are—as negative or depressing. She knew that bright utopian ideals frequently glow behind grim dystopian visions. "[Chekhov] has been called a pessimist," she writes in *Social Significance,* "as if one could miss the sun without feeling the torture of utter darkness!" She knew that torture in her own life, but she was not afraid: **"For where there is nothing, there man begins."**

ACKNOWLEDGEMENT

My thanks to colleague Paul Avrich, for bringing Emma Goldman's book to my attention.

H.G.C.

NOTES

1. S.N. Behrman, "Double Chocolate With Emma and Sasha," *The New Yorker*, January 16, 1954, p. 24.

2. See Richard Drinnon's informative chapter, "Popularizer of the Arts," in his biography of Goldman, *Rebel in Paradise* (Chicago: University of Chicago Press, 1961) pp. 155-164.

3. *Living My Life* (New York: Knopf, 1931; Dover Paperbound edition, two vols, 1970).

4. Alice Wexler, *Emma Goldman in America* (Boston: Beacon Press, 1984), p. 205.

5. Co-authored by Yeats with Lady Gregory, *Where There is Nothing* (1904) was later excluded by the poet from his collected works.

THE SOCIAL SIGNIFICANCE OF MODERN DRAMA

Library of Congress Cataloging-in-Publication Data

Goldman, Emma, 1869–1940.
    The social significance of modern drama.

    Bibliography: p.
    1. Drama—Social aspects. 2. European drama—History and criticism.
I. Title.
PN1643.G6   1987   809.2'9355   87–18816
ISBN 0–936839–62–7
ISBM 0–936839–61–9 (pbk.)

Distributed in U.K. and Europe by Applause Theatre Books Ltd., 9 Bow
Street, London, WC11.

APPLAUSE THEATRE BOOK PUBLISHERS
211 West 71st Street
New York, NY 10023
212/595-4735

Printed in the U.S.A.
First Applause Printing, 1987

TABLE OF CONTENTS

FOREWORD

In order to understand the social and dynamic significance of modern dramatic art it is necessary, I believe, to ascertain the difference between the functions of art for art's sake and art as the mirror of life.

Art for art's sake presupposes an attitude of aloofness on the part of the artist toward the complex struggle of life: he must rise above the ebb and tide of life. He is to be merely an artistic conjurer of beautiful forms, a creator of pure fancy.

That is not the attitude of modern art, which is preëminently the reflex, the mirror of life. The artist being a part of life cannot detach himself from the events and occurrences that pass panorama-like before his eyes, impressing themselves upon his emotional and intellectual vision.

The modern artist is, in the words of August Strindberg, "a lay preacher popularizing the pressing questions of his time." Not necessarily because his aim is to proselyte, but because he can best express himself by being true to life.

Millet, Meunier, Turgenev, Dostoyevsky, Emerson, Walt Whitman, Tolstoy, Ibsen, Strindberg, Hauptmann and a host of others mirror in their work as much of the spiritual and social revolt as is expressed by the most fiery speech of the propagandist. And more important still, they compel far greater attention. Their creative genius, imbued with the spirit of sincerity and truth, strikes root where the ordinary word often falls on barren soil.

The reason that many radicals as well as conservatives fail to grasp the powerful message of art is perhaps not far to seek. The average radical is as hidebound by mere terms as the man devoid of all ideas. "Bloated plutocrats," "economic determinism," "class consciousness," and similar expressions sum up for him the symbols of revolt. But since art speaks a language of its own, a language embracing the entire gamut of human emotions, it often sounds meaningless to those whose hearing has been dulled by the din of stereotyped phrases.

On the other hand, the conservative sees danger only in the advocacy of the Red Flag. He has too long been fed on the historic legend that it is only the "rabble" which makes revolutions, and not those who wield the brush or pen. It is therefore legitimate to applaud the artist and hound the rabble. Both radical and conservative have to learn that any mode of creative work, which with true perception portrays social wrongs earnestly and boldly, may be a greater menace to our social fabric and a more powerful inspiration than the wildest harangue of the soapbox orator.

Unfortunately, we in America have so far looked upon the theater as a place of amusement only, exclusive of ideas and inspiration. Because the modern drama of Europe has till recently been inaccessible in printed form to the average theatergoer in this country, he had to content himself with the interpretation, or rather misinterpretation, of our dramatic critics. As a result the social significance of the Modern Drama has well nigh been lost to the general public.

As to the native drama, America has so far produced very little worthy to be considered in a social light. Lacking the cultural and evolutionary tradition of the Old World, America has necessarily first to prepare the soil out of which sprouts creative genius.

The hundred and one springs of local and sectional life must have time to furrow their common channel into the seething sea of life at large, and social questions and problems make themselves felt, if not crystallized, before the throbbing pulse of the big national heart can find its reflex in a great literature—and specifically in the drama—of a social character. This evolution has been going on in this country for a considerable time, shaping the widespread unrest that is now beginning to assume more or less definite social form and expression.

Therefore, America could not so far produce its own social drama. But in proportion as the crystallization progresses, and sectional and national questions become clarified as fundamentally social problems, the drama develops. Indeed, very commendable beginnings in this direction have been made within recent years, among them "The Easiest Way," by Eugene Walter, "Keeping Up Appearances," and other plays by Butler Davenport, "Nowadays" and two other volumes of one-act plays, by George Middleton, —attempts that hold out an encouraging promise for the future.

The Modern Drama, as all modern literature, mirrors the complex struggle of life,—the struggle which, whatever its individual or topical expression, ever has its roots in the depth of human nature and social environment, and hence is, to that extent, universal. Such literature, such drama, is at once the reflex and the inspiration of mankind in its eternal seeking for things higher and better. Perhaps those who learn the great truths of the social travail in the school of life, do not need the message of the drama. But there is another class whose number is legion, for whom that message is indispensable. In countries where political oppression affects all classes, the best intellectual element have made common cause with the people, have become their teachers, comrades, and spokesmen. But in America political pressure has so far affected only the "common" people. It is they who are thrown into prison; they who are persecuted and mobbed, tarred and deported. Therefore another medium is needed to arouse the intellectuals of this country, to make them realize their relation to the people, to the social unrest permeating the atmosphere.

The medium which has the power to do that is the Modern Drama, because it mirrors every phase of life and embraces every strata of society,—the Modern Drama, showing each and all caught in the throes of the tremendous changes going on, and forced either to become part of the process or be left behind.

Ibsen, Strindberg, Hauptmann, Tolstoy, Shaw, Galsworthy and the other dramatists contained in this volume represent the social iconoclasts of our time. They know that society has gone beyond the stage of patching up, and that man must throw off the dead weight of the past, with all its ghosts and spooks, if he is to go foot free to meet the future.

This is the social significance which differentiates modern dramatic art from art for art's sake. It is the dynamite which undermines superstition, shakes the social pillars, and prepares men and women for the reconstruction.

THE SOCIAL SIGNIFICANCE
OF MODERN DRAMA

THE SCANDINAVIAN DRAMA

HENRIK IBSEN

In a letter to George Brandes, shortly after the Paris Commune, Henrik Ibsen wrote concerning the State and political liberty: "The State is the curse of the individual. How has the national strength of Prussia been purchased? By the sinking of the individual in a political and geographical formula. . . . The State must go! That will be a revolution which will find me on its side. Undermine the idea of the State, set up in its place spontaneous action, and the idea that spiritual relationship is the only thing that makes for unity, and you will start the elements of a liberty which will be something worth possessing."

The State was not the only *bête noire* of Henrik Ibsen. Every other institution which, like the State, rests upon a lie, was an iniquity to him. Uncompromising demolisher of all false idols and dynamiter of all social shams and hypocrisy, Ibsen consistently strove to uproot every stone of our social structure. Above all did he thunder his fiery indictment against the four cardinal sins of modern society: the Lie inherent in our social arrangements; Sacrifice and Duty, the twin curses that fetter the spirit of man; the narrow-mindedness and pettiness of Provincialism, that stifles all growth; and the Lack of Joy and Purpose in Work which turns life into a vale of misery and tears.

So strongly did Ibsen feel on these matters, that in none of his works did he lose sight of them. Indeed, they recur again and again, like a *Leitmotif* in music, in everything he wrote. These issues form the keynote to the revolutionary significance of his dramatic works, as well as to the psychology of Henrik Ibsen himself.

It is, therefore, not a little surprising that most of the interpreters and admirers of Ibsen so enthusiastically accept his art, and yet remain utterly indifferent to, not to say ignorant of, the message contained in it. That is mainly because they are, in the words of Mrs. Alving, "so pitifully afraid of the light." Hence they go about seeking mysteries and hunting symbols, and completely losing sight of the meaning that is as clear as daylight in all of the

5

works of Ibsen, and mainly in the group of his social plays, "The Pillars of Society," "A Doll's House," "Ghosts," and "An Enemy of the People."

THE PILLARS OF SOCIETY

The disintegrating effect of the Social Lie, of Duty, as an imposition and outrage, and of the spirit of Provincialism, as a stifling factor, are brought out with dynamic force in "The Pillars of Society."

Consul Bernick, driven by the conception of his duty toward the House of Bernick, begins his career with a terrible lie. He sells his love for *Lona Hessel* in return for the large dowry of her step-sister *Betty,* whom he does not love. To forget his treachery, he enters into a clandestine relationship with an actress of the town. When surprised in her room by the drunken husband, young *Bernick* jumps out of the window, and then graciously accepts the offer of his bosom friend, *Johan,* to let him take the blame.

Johan, together with his faithful sister *Lona,* leaves for America. In return for his devotion, young *Bernick* helps to rob his friend of his good name, by acquiescing in the rumors circulating in the town that *Johan* had broken into the safe of the *Bernicks* and stolen a large sum of money.

In the opening scene of "The Pillars of Society," we find *Consul Bernick* at the height of his career. The richest, most powerful and respected citizen of the community, he is held up as the model of an ideal husband and devoted father. In short, a worthy pillar of society.

The best ladies of the town come together in the home of the Bernicks. They represent the society for the "Lapsed and Lost," and they gather to do a little charitable sewing and a lot of charitable gossip. It is through them we learn that *Dina Dorf,* the ward of *Bernick,* is the issue of the supposed escapade of *Johan* and the actress.

With them, giving unctuous spiritual advice and representing the purity and morality of the community, is *Rector Rorlund,* hidebound, self-righteous, and narrow-minded.

Into this deadening atmosphere of mental and social provincialism comes *Lona Hessel,* refreshing and invigorating as the wind of the plains. She has returned to her native town together with *Johan.*

The moment she enters the house of *Bernick,* the whole structure begins to totter. For in *Lona's* own words, "Fie, fie—this moral linen here smells so

tainted—just like a shroud. I am accustomed to the air of the prairies now, I can tell you. . . . Wait a little, wait a little—we'll soon rise from the sepulcher. We must have broad daylight here when my boy comes."
Broad daylight is indeed needed in the community of *Consul Bernick,* and above all in the life of the *Consul* himself.

It seems to be the psychology of a lie that it can never stand alone. *Consul Bernick* is compelled to weave a network of lies to sustain his foundation. In the disguise of a good husband, he upbraids, nags, and tortures his wife on the slightest provocation. In the mask of a devoted father, he tyrannizes and bullies his only child as only a despot used to being obeyed can do. Under the cloak of a benevolent citizen he buys up public land for his own profit. Posing as a true Christian, he even goes so far as to jeopordize human life. Because of business considerations he sends *The Indian Girl,* an unseaworthy, rotten vessel, on a voyage, although he is assured by one of his most capable and faithful workers that the ship cannot make the journey, that it is sure to go down. But *Consul Bernick* is a pillar of society; he needs the respect and good will of his fellow citizens. He must go from precipice to precipice, to keep up appearances.

Lona alone sees the abyss facing him, and tells him: "What does it matter whether such a society is supported or not? What is it that passes current here? Lies and shams—nothing else. Here are you, the first man in the town, living in wealth and pride, in power and honor, you, who have set the brand of crime upon an innocent man." She might have added, *many* innocent men, for *Johan* was not the only one at whose expense *Karsten Bernick* built up his career.

The end is inevitable. In the words of *Lona:* "All this eminence, and you yourself along with it, stand on a trembling quicksand; a moment may come, a word may be spoken, and, if you do not save yourself in time, you and your whole grandeur go to the bottom."

But for *Lona,* or, rather, what she symbolizes, *Bernick*—even as *The Indian Girl*—would go to the bottom.

In the last act, the whole town is preparing to give the great philanthropist and benefactor, the eminent pillar of society, an ovation. There are fireworks, music, gifts and speeches in honor of *Consul Bernick.* At that very moment, the only child of the *Consul* is hiding in *The Indian Girl* to escape the tyranny of his home. *Johan,* too, is supposed to sail on the same ship, and with him, *Dina,* who has learned the whole truth and is eager to escape from her prison, to go to a free atmosphere, to become independent, and then to unite with *Johan* in love and freedom. As *Dina* says: "Yes, I will be your wife. But first I will work, and become something for myself, just as you are. I will give myself, I will not be taken."

Consul Bernick, too, is beginning to realize himself. The strain of events and the final shock that he had exposed his own child to such peril, act like a stroke of lightning on the *Consul.* It makes him see that a house built on lies, shams, and crime must eventually sink by its own weight. Surrounded by those who truly love and therefore understand him, *Consul Bernick,* no longer the pillar of society, but the man becomes conscious of his better self.

"Where have I been?" he exclaims. "You will be horrified when you know. Now, I feel as if I had just recovered my senses after being poisoned. But I feel—I feel that I *can* be young and strong again. Oh, come nearer— closer around me. Come, Betty! Come, Olaf! Come, Martha! Oh, Martha, it seems as though I had never seen you in all these years. And we—we have a long, earnest day of work before us; I most of all. But let it come; gather close around me, you true and faithful women. I have learned this, in these days: it is you women who are the Pillars of Society."

Lona: "Then you have learned a poor wisdom, brother-in-law. No, no; the spirit of Truth and of Freedom—these are the Pillars of Society."

The spirit of truth and freedom is the sociorevolutionary significance of "The Pillars of Society." Those, who, like *Consul Bernick,* fail to realize this all-important fact, go on patching up *The Indian Girl,* which is Ibsen's symbol for our society. But they, too, must learn that society is rotten to the core; that patching up or reforming one sore spot merely drives the social poison deeper into the system, and that all must go to the bottom unless the spirit of Truth and Freedom revolutionize the world.

A DOLL'S HOUSE

In "A Doll's House" Ibsen returns to the subject so vital to him,—the Social Lie and Duty,—this time as manifesting themselves in the sacred institution of the home and in the position of woman in her gilded cage.

Nora is the beloved, adored wife of *Torvald Helmer.* He is an admirable man, rigidly honest, of high moral ideals, and passionately devoted to his wife and children. In short, a good man and an enviable husband. Almost every mother would be proud of such a match for her daughter, and the latter would consider herself fortunate to become the wife of such a man. *Nora,* too, considers herself fortunate. Indeed, she worships her husband, believes in him implicitly, and is sure that if ever her safety should be menaced, *Torvald,* her idol, her god, would perform the miracle. When a woman loves as *Nora* does, nothing else matters; least of all, social, legal or moral considerations. Therefore, when her husband's life is threatened, it is no effort, it is joy for *Nora* to forge her father's name to a note and borrow 800 cronen on it, in order to take her sick husband to Italy.

In her eagerness to serve her husband, and in perfect innocence of the legal aspect of her act, she does not give the matter much thought, except for her anxiety to shield him from any emergency that may call upon him to perform the miracle in her behalf. She works hard, and saves every penny of her pin-money to pay back the amount she borrowed on the forged check.

Nora is light-hearted and gay, apparently without depth. Who, indeed, would expect depth of a doll, a "squirrel," a song-bird? Her purpose in life is to be happy for her husband's sake, for the sake of the children; to sing, dance, and play with them. Besides, is she not shielded, protected, and cared for? Who, then, would suspect *Nora* of depth? But already in the opening scene, when *Torvald* inquires what his precious "squirrel" wants for a Christmas present, *Nora* quickly asks him for money. Is it to buy macaroons or finery? In her talk with *Mrs. Linden, Nora* reveals her inner self, and forecasts the inevitable debacle of her doll's house.

After telling her friend how she had saved her husband, *Nora* says: "When Torvald gave me money for clothes and so on, I never used more than half of it; I always bought the simplest things. . . . Torvald never noticed anything. But it was often very hard, Christina dear. For it's nice to be beautifully dressed. Now, isn't it? . . . Well, and besides that, I made money in other ways. Last winter I was so lucky—I got a heap of copying to do. I shut myself up every evening and wrote far into the night. Oh, sometimes I was so tired, so tired. And yet it was splendid to work in that way and earn money. I almost felt as if I was a man.

Down deep in the consciousness of *Nora* there evidently slumbers personality and character, which could come into full bloom only through a great miracle—not the kind *Nora* hopes for, but a miracle just the same.

Nora had borrowed the money from *Nils Krogstad,* a man with a shady past in the eyes of the community and of the righteous moralist, *Torvald*

Helmer. So long as *Krogstad* is allowed the little breathing space a Christian people grants to him who has once broken its laws, he is reasonably human. He does not molest *Nora.* But when *Helmer* becomes director of the bank in which *Krogstad* is employed, and threatens the man with dismissal, *Krogstad* naturally fights back. For as he says to *Nora:* "If need be, I shall fight as though for my life to keep my little place in the bank. . . . It's not only for the money: that matters least to me. It's something else. Well, I'd better make a clean breast of it. Of course you know, like every one else, that some years ago I—got into trouble. . . . The matter never came into court; but from that moment all paths were barred to me. Then I took up the business you know about. I was obliged to grasp at something; and I don't think I've been one of the worst. But now I must clear out of it all. My sons are growing up; for their sake I must try to win back as much respectability as I can. This place in the bank was the first step, and now your husband wants to kick me off the ladder, back into the mire. Mrs. Helmer, you evidently have no clear idea what you have really done. But I can assure you that it was nothing more and nothing worse that made me an outcast from society. . . . But this I may tell you, that if I'm flung into the gutter a second time, you shall keep me company."

Even when *Nora* is confronted with this awful threat, she does not fear for herself, only for *Torvald,*—so good, so true, who has such an aversion to debts, but who loves her so devotedly that for her sake he would take the blame upon himself. But this must never be. *Nora,* too, begins a fight for life, for her husband's life and that of her children. Did not *Helmer* tell her that the very presence of a criminal like *Krogstad* poisons the children? And is she not a criminal?

Torvald Helmer assures her, in his male conceit, that "early corruption generally comes from the mother's side, but of course the father's influence may act in the same way. And this Krogstad has been poisoning his own children for years past by a life of lies and hypocrisy—that's why I call him morally ruined."

Poor *Nora,* who cannot understand why a daughter has no right to spare her dying father anxiety, or why a wife has no right to save her husband's life, is surely not aware of the true character of her idol. But gradually the veil is lifted. At first, when in reply to her desperate pleading for *Krogstad,* her husband discloses the true reason for wanting to get rid of him: "The fact is, he was a college chum of mine—there was one of those rash friendships between us that one so often repents later. I don't mind confessing it—he calls me by my Christian name; and he insists on doing it even when others are present. He delights in putting on airs of familiarity—Torvald here, Torvald there! I assure you it's most painful to me. He would make my position at the bank perfectly unendurable."

And then again when the final blow comes. For forty-eight hours *Nora* battles for her ideal, never doubting *Torvald* for a moment. Indeed, so absolutely sure is she of her strong oak, her lord, her god, that she would rather kill herself than have him take the blame for her act. The end comes, and with it the doll's house tumbles down, and *Nora* discards her doll's dress— she sheds her skin, as it were. *Torvald Helmer* proves himself a petty Philistine, a bully and a coward, as so many good husbands when they throw off their respectable cloak.

Helmer's rage over *Nora's* crime subsides the moment the danger of publicity is averted—proving that *Helmer,* like many a moralist, is not so much incensed at *Nora's* offense as by the fear of being found out. Not so *Nora.* Finding out is her salvation. It is then that she realizes how much she has been wronged, that she is only a plaything, a doll to *Helmer.* In her disillusionment she says, "You have never loved me. You only thought it amusing to be in love with me."

Helmer. Why, Nora, what a thing to say!

Nora. Yes, it is so, Torvald. While I was at home with father he used to tell me all his opinions and I held the same opinions. If I had others I concealed them, because he would not have liked it. He used to call me his doll child, and play with me as I played with my dolls. Then I came to live in your house— . . . I mean I passed from father's hands into yours. You settled everything according to your taste; and I got the same tastes as you; or I pretended to—I don't know which—both ways perhaps. When I look back on it now, I seem to have been living here like a beggar, from hand to mouth. I lived by performing tricks for you, Torvald. But you would have it so. You and father have done me a great wrong. It's your fault that my life has been wasted. . . .

Helmer. It's exasperating! Can you forsake your holiest duties in this way?

Nora. What do you call my holiest duties?

Helmer. Do you ask me that? Your duties to your husband and your children.

Nora. I have other duties equally sacred.

Helmer. Impossible! What duties do you mean?

Nora. My duties toward myself.

Helmer. Before all else you are a wife and a mother.

Nora. That I no longer believe. I think that before all else I am a human being, just as much as you are—or, at least, I will try to become one. I know that most people agree with you, Torvald, and that they say so in books. But henceforth I can't be satisfied with what most people say, and what is in books. I must think things out for myself and try to get clear about them. . . . I had been living here these eight years with a strange man, and had borne him three children—Oh! I can't bear to think of it—I could tear myself to pieces! . . . I can't spend the night in a strange man's house.

Is there anything more degrading to woman than to live with a stranger, and bear him children? Yet, the lie of the marriage institution decrees that she shall continue to do so, and the social conception of duty insists that for the sake of that lie she need be nothing else than a plaything, a doll, a nonentity.

When *Nora* closes behind her the door of her doll's house, she opens wide the gate of life for woman, and proclaims the revolutionary message that only perfect freedom and communion make a true bond between man and woman, meeting in the open, without lies, without shame, free from the bondage of duty.

GHOSTS

The social and revolutionary significance of Henrik Ibsen is brought out with even greater force in "Ghosts" than in his preceding works.

Not only does this pioneer of modern dramatic art undermine in "Ghosts" the Social Lie and the paralyzing effect of Duty, but the uselessness and evil of Sacrifice, the dreary Lack of Joy and of Purpose in Work are brought to light as most pernicious and destructive elements in life.

Mrs. Alving, having made what her family called a most admirable match, discovers shortly after her marriage that her husband is a drunkard and a *roué.* In her despair she flees to her young friend, the divinity student *Manders.* But he, preparing to save souls, even though they be encased in rotten bodies, sends *Mrs. Alving* back to her husband and her duties toward her home.

Helen Alving is young and immature. Besides, she loves young *Manders;* his command is law to her. She returns home, and for twenty-five years suffers all the misery and torture of the damned. That she survives is due mainly to her passionate love for the child born of that horrible relationship—her boy *Oswald,* her all in life. He must be saved at any cost. To do that, she had sacrificed her great yearning for him and sent him away from the poisonous atmosphere of her home.

And now he has returned, fine and free, much to the disgust of *Pastor Manders,* whose limited vision cannot conceive that out in the large world free men and women can live a decent and creative life.

Manders. But how is it possible that a—a young man or young woman with any decent principles can endure to live in that way?—in the eyes of all the world!

Oswald. What are they to do? A poor young artist—a poor girl. It costs a lot of money to get married. What are they to do?

Manders. What are they to do? Let me tell you, Mr. Alving, what they ought to do. They ought to exercise self-restraint from the first; that's what they ought to do.

Oswald. Such talk as that won't go far with warm-blooded young people, over head and ears in love.

Mrs. Alving. No, it wouldn't go far.

Manders. How can the authorities tolerate such things? Allow it to go on in the light of day? (*To Mrs. Alving.*) Had I not cause to be deeply concerned about your son? In circles where open immorality prevails, and has even a sort of prestige—!

Oswald. Let me tell you, sir, that I have been a constant Sunday-guest in one or two such irregular homes—

Manders. On Sunday of all days!

Oswald. Isn't that the day to enjoy one's self? Well, never have I heard an offensive word, and still less have I ever witnessed anything that could be called immoral. No; do you know when and where I have found immorality in artistic circles?

Manders. No! Thank heaven, I don't!

Oswald. Well, then, allow me to inform you. I have met with it when one or other of our pattern husbands and fathers has come to Paris to have a look around on his own account, and has done the artists the honor of visiting their humble haunts. *They* knew what was what. These gentlemen could tell us all about places and things we had never dreamt of.

Manders. What? Do you mean to say that respectable men from home here would—?

Oswald. Have you never heard these respectable men, when they got home again, talking about the way in which immorality was running rampant abroad?

Manders. Yes, of course.

Mrs. Alving. I have, too.

Oswald. Well, you may take their word for it. They know what they are talking about! Oh! that that great, free, glorious life out there should be defiled in such a way!

Pastor Manders is outraged, and when *Oswald* leaves, he delivers himself of a tirade against *Mrs. Alving* for her "irresponsible proclivities to shirk her duty."

Manders. It is only the spirit of rebellion that craves for happiness in this life. What right have we human beings to happiness? No, we have to do our duty! And your duty was to hold firmly to the man you had once chosen and to whom you were bound by a holy tie. . . . It was your duty to bear with humility the cross which a Higher Power had, for your own good, laid upon you. But instead of that you rebelliously cast away the cross. . . . I was but a poor instrument in a Higher Hand. And what a blessing has it not been to you all the days of your life, that I got you to resume the yoke of duty and obedience!

The price *Mrs. Alving* had to pay for her yoke, her duty and obedience, staggers even *Dr. Manders,* when she reveals to him the martyrdom she had endured those long years.

Mrs. Alving. You have now spoken out, Pastor Manders; and to-morrow you are to speak publicly in memory of my husband. I shall not speak to-morrow. But now I will speak out a little to you, as you have spoken to me. . . . I want you to know that after nineteen years of marriage my husband remained as dissolute in his desires as he was when you married us. After Oswald's birth, I thought Alving seemed to be a little better. But it did not last long. And then I had to struggle twice as hard, fighting for life or death, so that nobody should know what sort of a man my child's father was. I had my little son to bear it for. But when the last insult was added; when my own servant-maid—Then I swore to myself: This shall come to an end. And so I took the upper hand in the house—the whole control over him and over everything else. For now I had a weapon against him, you see; he dared not oppose me. It was then that Oswald was sent from home. He was in his seventh year, and was beginning to observe and ask questions, as children do. That I could not bear. I thought the child must get poisoned by merely breathing the air in this polluted home. That was why I placed him out. And now you can see, too, why he was never allowed to set foot inside his home so long as his father lived. No one knows what it has cost me. . . . From the day after to-morrow it shall be for me as though he who is dead had never lived in this house. No one shall be here but my boy and his mother. *(From within the dining-room comes the noise of a chair overturned, and at the same moment is heard:)*

Regina *(sharply, but whispering).* Oswald! take care! are you mad? let me go!

Mrs. Alving *(starts in terror).* Ah! *(She stares wildly toward the half-opened door. Oswald is heard coughing and humming inside).*

Manders *(excited).* What in the world is the matter? What is it, Mrs. Alving?

Mrs. Alving *(hoarsely).* Ghosts! The couple from the conservatory has risen again!

Ghosts, indeed! *Mrs. Alving* sees this but too clearly when she discovers that though she did not want *Oswald* to inherit a single penny from the purchase money *Captain Alving* had paid for her, all her sacrifice did not save *Oswald* from the poisoned heritage of his father. She learns soon enough that her beloved boy had inherited a terrible disease from his father, as a result of which he will never again be able to work. She also finds out that, for all her freedom, she has remained in the clutches of Ghosts, and that she has fostered in *Oswald's* mind an ideal of his father, the more terrible because of her own loathing for the man. Too late she realizes her fatal mistake:

Mrs. Alving. I ought never to have concealed the facts of Alving's life. But . . . in my superstitious awe for Duty and Decency I lied to my boy, year after year. Oh! what a coward, what a coward I have been! . . . Ghosts! When I heard Regina and Oswald in there, it was as though I saw the Ghosts before me. But I almost think we are all of us Ghosts, Pastor Manders. It is not only what we have inherited from our father and mother that "walks" in us. It is all sorts of dead ideas, and lifeless old beliefs, and so forth. They have no vitality, but they cling to us all the same, and we can't get rid of them. . . . There must be Ghosts all the country over, as thick as the sand of the sea. And then we are, one and all, so pitifully afraid of the light. . . . When you forced me under the yoke you called Duty and Obligation; when you praised as right and proper what my whole soul rebelled against, as something loathsome. It was then that I began to look into the seams of your doctrine. I only wished to pick at a single knot; but when I had got that undone, the whole thing ravelled out. And then I understood that it was all machine-sewn. . . . It was a crime against us both.

Indeed, a crime on which the sacred institution is built, and for which thousands of innocent children must pay with their happiness and life, while their mothers continue to the very end without ever learning how hideously criminal their life is.

Not so *Mrs. Alving* who, though at a terrible price, works herself out to the truth; aye, even to the height of understanding the dissolute life of the father of her child, who had lived in cramped provincial surroundings, and could find no purpose in life, no outlet for his exuberance. It is through her child, through *Oswald,* that all this becomes illumed to her.

Oswald. Ah, the joy of life, mother; that's a thing you don't know much about in these parts. I have never felt it here. . . . And then, too, the joy of work. At bottom, it's the same thing. But that too you know nothing about. . . . Here people are brought up to believe that work is a curse and a punishment for sin, and that life is something miserable, something we want to be done with, the sooner the better. . . . Have you noticed that everything I have painted has turned upon the joy of life? always, always upon the joy of life?—light and sunshine and glorious air, and faces radiant with happiness? That is why I am afraid of remaining at home with you.

Mrs. Alving. Oswald, you spoke of the joy of life; and at that word a new light burst for me over my life and all it has contained. . . . You ought to have known your father when he was a young lieutenant. He was brimming over with the joy of life! . . . He had no object in life, but only an official position. He had no work into which he could throw himself heart and soul; he had only business. He had not a single comrade that knew what the joy of life meant—only loafers and boon companions— . . . So that happened which was sure to happen. . . . Oswald, my dear boy; has it shaken you very much?

Oswald. Of course it came upon me as a great surprise, but, after all, it can't matter much to me.

Mrs. Alving. Can't matter! That your father was so infinitely miserable!

Oswald. Of course I can pity him as I would anybody else; but—

Mrs. Alving. Nothing more? Your own father!

Oswald. Oh, there! "Father," "father"! I never knew anything of father. I don't remember anything about him except—that he once made me sick.

Mrs. Alving. That's a terrible way to speak! Should not a son love his father, all the same?

Oswald. When a son has nothing to thank his father for? has never known him? Do you really cling to the old superstition?—you who are so enlightened in other ways?

Mrs. Alving. Is that only a superstition?

In truth, a superstition—one that is kept like the sword of Damocles over the child who does not ask to be given life, and is yet tied with a thousand chains to those who bring him into a cheerless, joyless, and wretched world. The voice of Henrik Ibsen in "Ghosts" sounds like the trumpets before the walls of Jericho. Into the remotest nooks and corners reaches his voice, with its thundering indictment of our moral cancers, our social poisons, our hideous crimes against unborn and born victims. Verily a more revolutionary condemnation has never been uttered in dramatic form before or since the great Henrik Ibsen.

We need, therefore, not be surprised at the vile abuse and denunciation heaped upon Ibsen's head by the Church, the State, and other moral eunuchs. But the spirit of Henrik Ibsen could not be daunted. It asserted itself with even greater defiance in "An Enemy of the People,"—a powerful arraignment of the political and economic Lie,—Ibsen's own confession of faith.

AN ENEMY OF THE PEOPLE

Dr. Thomas Stockmann is called to the position of medical adviser to the management of the "Baths," the main resource of his native town.

A sincere man of high ideals, *Dr. Stockmann* returns home after an absence of many years, full of the spirit of enterprise and progressive innovation. For as he says to his brother *Peter*, the town *Burgomaster*, "I am so glad and content. I feel so unspeakably happy in the midst of all this growing, germinating life. After all, what a glorious time we do live in. It is as if a new world were springing up around us."

Burgomaster. Do you really think so?

Dr. Stockmann. Well, of course, you can't see this as clearly as I do. You've spent all your life in this place, and so your perceptions have been dulled. But I, who had to live up there in that small hole in the north all those years, hardly ever seeing a soul to speak a stimulating word to me—all this affects me as if I were carried to the midst of a crowded city—I know well enough that the conditions of life are small compared with many other towns. But here is life, growth, an infinity of things to work for and to strive for; and that is the main point.

In this spirit *Dr. Stockmann* sets to his task. After two years of careful investigation, he finds that the Baths are built on a swamp, full of poisonous germs, and that people who come there for their health will be infected with fever.

Thomas Stockmann is a conscientious physician. He loves his native town, but he loves his fellow-men more. He considers it his duty to communicate his discovery to the highest authority of the town, the *Burgomaster*, his brother *Peter Stockmann*.

Dr. Stockmann is indeed an idealist; else he would know that the man is often lost in the official. Besides, *Peter Stockmann* is also the president of the board of directors and one of the heaviest stockholders of the Baths. Sufficient reason to upbraid his reckless medical brother as a dangerous man:

Burgomaster. Anyhow, you've an ingrained propensity for going your own way. And that in a well-ordered community is almost as dangerous. The individual must submit himself to the whole community, or, to speak more correctly, bow to the authority that watches over the welfare of all.

But the *Doctor* is not disconcerted: *Peter* is an official; he is not concerned with ideals. But there is the press,—that is the medium for his purpose! The staff of the *People's Messenger—Hovstad, Billings,* and *Aslaksen,* are deeply impressed by the *Doctor's* discovery. With one eye to good copy and the other to the political chances, they immediately put the *People's Messenger* at the disposal of *Thomas Stockmann. Hovstad* sees great possibilities for a thorough radical reform of the whole life of the community.

Hovstad. To you, as a doctor and a man of science, this business of the water-works is an isolated affair. I fancy it hasn't occurred to you that a good many other things are connected with it. . . . The swamp our whole municipal life stands and rots in. . . . I think a journalist assumes an immense responsibility when he neglects an opportunity of aiding the masses, the poor, the oppressed. I know well enough that the upper classes will call this stirring up the people, and so forth, but they can do as they please, if only my conscience is clear.

Aslaksen, printer of the *People's Messenger,* chairman of the Householders' Association, and agent for the Moderation Society, has, like *Hovstad,* a keen eye to business. He assures the *Doctor* of his whole-hearted coöperation, especially emphasizing that, "It might do you no harm to have us middle-class men at your back. We now form a compact majority in the town—when we really make up our minds to. And it's always as well, Doctor, to have the majority with you. . . . And so I think it wouldn't be amiss if we made some sort of a demonstration. . . . Of course with great moderation, Doctor. I am always in favor of moderation; for moderation is a citizen's first virtue—at least those are my sentiments."

Truly, *Dr. Stockmann* is an idealist; else he would not place so much faith in the staff of the *People's Messenger,* who love the people so well that they constantly feed them with high-sounding phrases of democratic principles and of the noble function of the press, while they pilfer their pockets.

That is expressed in *Hovstad's* own words, when *Petra,* the daughter of *Dr. Stockmann,* returns a sentimental novel she was to translate for the *People's Messenger:* "This can't possibly go into the *Messenger,*" she tells Hovstad; "it is in direct contradiction to your own opinion."

Hovstad. Well, but for the sake of the cause—

Petra. You don't understand me yet. It is all about a supernatural power that looks after the so-called good people here on earth, and turns all things to their advantage at last, and all the bad people are punished.

Hovstad. Yes, but that's very fine. It's the very thing the public like.

Petra. And would you supply the public with such stuff? Why, you don't believe one word of it yourself. You know well enough that things don't really happen like that.

Hovstad. You're right there; but an editor can't always do as he likes. He often has to yield to public opinion in small matters. After all, politics is the chief thing in life—at any rate for a newspaper; and if I want the people to follow me along the path of emancipation and progress, I mustn't scare them away. If they find such a moral story down in the cellar, they're much more willing to stand what is printed above it—they feel themselves safer.

Editors of the stamp of *Hovstad* seldom dare to express their real opinions. They cannot afford to "scare away" their readers. They generally yield to the most ignorant and vulgar public opinion; they do not set themselves up against constituted authority. Therefore the *People's Messenger* drops the "greatest man" in town when it learns that the *Burgomaster* and the influential citizens are determined that the truth shall be silenced. The *Burgomaster* soundly denounces his brother's "rebellion."

Burgomaster. The public doesn't need new ideas. The public is best served by the good old recognized ideas that they have already. . . . As an official, you've no right to have any individual conviction.

Dr. Stockmann. The source is poisoned, man! Are you mad? We live by trafficking in filth and garbage. The whole of our developing social life is rooted in a lie!

Burgomaster. Idle fancies—or something worse. The man who makes such offensive insinuations against his own native place must be an enemy of society.

Dr. Stockmann. And I must bear such treatment! In my own house. Katrine! What do you think of it?

Mrs. Stockmann. Indeed, it is a shame and an insult, Thomas— . . . But, after all, your brother has the power—

Dr. Stockmann. Yes, but I have the right!

Mrs. Stockmann. Ah, yes, right, right! What is the good of being right when you haven't any might?

Dr. Stockmann. What! No good in a free society to have right on your side? You are absurd, Katrine. And besides, haven't I the free and independent press with me? The compact majority behind me? That's might enough, I should think!

Katrine Stockmann is wiser than her husband. For he who has no might need hope for no right. The good *Doctor* has to drink the bitter cup to the last drop before he realizes the wisdom of his wife.

Threatened by the authorities and repudiated by the *People's Messenger,* *Dr. Stockmann* attempts to secure a hall wherein to hold a public meeting. A free-born citizen, he believes in the Constitution and its guarantees; he is determined to maintain his right of free expression. But like so many others, even most advanced liberals blinded by the spook of constitutional rights and free speech, *Dr. Stockmann* inevitably has to pay the penalty of his credulity. He finds every hall in town closed against him. Only one solitary citizen has the courage to open his doors to the persecuted Doctor,—his old friend *Horster.* But the mob follows him even there and howls him down as an enemy of society. *Thomas Stockmann* makes the discovery in his battle with ignorance, stupidity, and vested interests that "the most dangerous enemies of truth and freedom in our midst are the compact majority, the damned compact liberal majority." His experiences lead him to the conclusion that "the majority is never right. . . . That is one of those conventional lies against which a free, thoughtful man must rebel. . . . The majority has might unhappily —but right it has not."

Hovstad. The man who would ruin a whole community must be an enemy of society!

Dr. Stockmann. It doesn't matter if a lying community is ruined! . . . You'll poison the whole country in time; you will bring it to such a pass that the whole country will deserve to perish. And should it come to this, I say, from the bottom of my heart: Perish the country! Perish all its people!

Driven out of the place, hooted and jeered by the mob, *Dr. Stockmann* barely escapes with his life, and seeks safety in his home, only to find everything demolished there. In due time he is repudiated by the grocer, the baker, and the candlestick maker. The landlord, of course, is very sorry for him. The Stockmanns have always paid their rent regularly, but it would injure his reputation to have such an avowed rebel for a tenant. The grocer is sorry, and the butcher, too; but they can not jeopardize their business. Finally the board of education sends expressions of regret: *Petra* is an excellent teacher and the boys of Stockmann splendid pupils, but it would contaminate the other children were the Stockmanns allowed to remain at school. And again *Dr. Stockmann* learns a vital lesson. But he will not submit; he will be strong.

Dr. Stockmann. Should I let myself be beaten off the field by public opinion, and the compact majority, and such deviltry? No, thanks. Besides, what I want is so simple, so clear and straightforward. I only want to drive into the heads of these curs that the Liberals are the worst foes of free men; that party-programmes wring the necks of all young living truths; that considerations of expediency turn morality and righteousness upside down, until life is simply hideous. . . . I don't see any man free and brave enough to dare the Truth. . . . The strongest man is he who stands most alone.

A confession of faith, indeed, because Henrik Ibsen, although recognized as a great dramatic artist, remained alone in his stand as a revolutionist.

STRINDBERG

"The reproach was levelled against my tragedy, 'The Father,' that it was so sad, as though one wanted merry tragedies. People clamour for the joy of life, and the theatrical managers order farces, as though the joy of life consisted in being foolish, and in describing people as if they were each and all afflicted with St. Vitus's dance or idiocy. I find the joy of life in the powerful, cruel struggle of life, and my enjoyment in discovering something, in learning something."

The passionate desire to discover something, to learn something, has made of August Strindberg a keen dissector of souls. Above all, of his own soul.

Surely there is no figure in contemporary literature, outside of Tolstoy, that laid bare the most secret nooks and corners of his own soul with the sincerity of August Strindberg. One so relentlessly honest with himself, could be no less with others.

That explains the bitter opposition and hatred of his critics. They did not object so much to Strindberg's self-torture; but that he should have dared to torture *them,* to hold up his searching mirror to *their* sore spots, that they could not forgive.

Especially is this true of woman. For centuries she has been lulled into a trance by the songs of the troubadours who paid homage to her goodness, her sweetness, her selflessness and, above all, her noble motherhood. And though she is beginning to appreciate that all this incense has befogged her mind and paralyzed her soul, she hates to give up the tribute laid at her feet by sentimental moonshiners of the past.

To be sure, it is rude to turn on the full searchlight upon a painted face. But how is one to know what is back of the paint and artifice? August Strindberg hated artifice with all the passion of his being; hence his severe criticism of woman. Perhaps it was his tragedy to see her as she really is, and not as she appears in her trance. To love with open eyes is, indeed, a tragedy, and Strindberg loved woman. All his life long he yearned for her love, as mother, as wife, as companion. But his longing for, and his need of her, were the crucible of Strindberg, as they have been the crucible of every man, even of the mightiest spirit.

Why it is so is best expressed in the words of the old nurse, *Margret,* in "The Father": "Because all you men, great and small, are woman's children, every man of you."

The child in man—and the greater the man the more dominant the child in him—has ever succumbed to the Earth Spirit, Woman, and as long as that is her only drawing power, Man, with all his strength and genius, will ever be at her feet. The Earth Spirit is motherhood carrying the race in its womb; the flame of life luring the moth, often against its will, to destruction. In all of Strindberg's plays we see the flame of life at work, ravishing man's brain, consuming man's faith, rousing man's passion. Always, always the flame of life is drawing its victims with irresistible force. August Strindberg's arraignment of that force is at the same time a confession of faith. He, too, was the child of woman, and utterly helpless before her.

THE FATHER

"The Father" portrays the tragedy of a man and a woman struggling for the possession of their child. The father, a cavalry captain, is intellectual, a freethinker, a man of ideas. His wife is narrow, selfish, and unscrupulous in her methods when her antagonism is wakened.

Other members of the family are the wife's mother, a Spiritualist, and the *Captain's* old nurse, *Margret,* ignorant and superstitious. The father feels that the child would be poisoned in such an atmosphere:

The Captain. This house is full of women who all want to have their say about my child. My mother-in-law wants to make a Spiritualist of her. Laura wants her to be an artist; the governess wants her to be a Methodist, old Margret a Baptist, and the servant-girls want her to join the Salvation Army! It won't do to try to make a soul in patches like that. I, who have the chief right to try to form her character, am constantly opposed in my efforts. And that's why I have decided to send her away from home.

But it is not only because the *Captain* does not believe in "making a soul in patches," that he wants to rescue the child from the hot-house environment, nor because he plans to make her an image of himself. It is rather because he wants her to grow up with a healthy outlook on life.

The Captain. I don't want to be a procurer for my daughter and educate her exclusively for matrimony, for then if she were left unmarried she might have bitter days. On the other hand, I don't want to influence her toward a career that requires a long course of training which would be entirely thrown away if she should marry. I want her to be a teacher. If she remains unmarried she will be able to support herself, and at any rate she wouldn't be any worse off than the poor schoolmasters who have to share their salaries with a family. If she marries she can use her knowledge in the education of her children.

While the father's love is concerned with the development of the child, that of the mother is interested mainly in the possession of the child. Therefore she fights the man with every means at her command, even to the point of instilling the poison of doubt into his mind, by hints that he is not the father of the child. Not only does she seek to drive her husband mad, but through skillful intrigue she leads every one, including the Doctor, to believe that he is actually insane. Finally even the old nurse is induced to betray him: she slips the straitjacket over him, adding the last touch to the treachery. Robbed of his faith, broken in spirit and subdued, the *Captain* dies a victim of the Earth Spirit—of motherhood, which slays the man for the sake of the child. Laura herself will have it so when she tells her husband, "You have fulfilled your function as an unfortunately necessary father and breadwinner. You are not needed any longer, and you must go."

Critics have pronounced "The Father" an aberration of Strindberg's mind, utterly false and distorted. But that is because they hate to face the truth. In Strindberg, however, the truth is his most revolutionary significance.

"The Father" contains two basic truths. Motherhood, much praised, poetized, and hailed as a wonderful thing, is in reality very often the greatest deterrent influence in the life of the child. Because it is not primarily concerned with the potentialities of character and growth of the child; on the contrary, it is interested chiefly in the birthgiver,—that is, the mother. Therefore, the mother is the most subjective, self-centered and conservative obstacle. She binds the child to herself with a thousand threads which never grant sufficient freedom for mental and spiritual expansion. It is not necessary to be as bitter as Strindberg to realize this. There are of course exceptional mothers who continue to grow with the child. But the average mother is like the hen with her brood, forever fretting about her chicks if they venture a step away from the coop. The mother enslaves with kindness,—a bondage harder to bear and more difficult to escape than the brutal fist of the father.

Strindberg himself experienced it, and nearly every one who has ever attempted to outgrow the soul strings of the mother.

In portraying motherhood, as it really is, August Strindberg is conveying a vital and revolutionary message, namely, that true motherhood, even as fatherhood, does not consist in molding the child according to one's image, or in imposing upon it one's own ideas and notions, but in allowing the child freedom and opportunity to grow harmoniously according to its own potentialities, unhampered and unmarred.

The child was August Strindberg's religion,—perhaps because of his own very tragic childhood and youth. He was like Father Time in "Jude the Obscure," a giant child, and as he has *Laura* say of the *Captain* in "The Father," "he had either come too early into the world, or perhaps was not wanted at all."

"Yes, that's how it was," the *Captain* replies, "my father's and my mother's will was against my coming into the world, and consequently I was born without a will."

The horror of having been brought into the world undesired and unloved, stamped its indelible mark on August Strindberg. It never left him. Nor did fear and hunger—the two terrible phantoms of his childhood.

Indeed, the child was Strindberg's religion, his faith, his passion. Is it then surprising that he should have resented woman's attitude towards the man as a mere means to the child; or, in the words of *Laura*, as "the function of father and breadwinner"? That this is the attitude of woman, is of course denied. But it is nevertheless true. It holds good not only of the average, unthinking woman, but even of many feminists of to-day; and, no doubt, they were even more antagonistic to the male in Strindberg's time.

It is only too true that woman is paying back what she has endured for centuries—humiliation, subjection, and bondage. But making oneself free through the enslavement of another, is by no means a step toward advancement. Woman must grow to understand that the father is as vital a factor in the life of the child as is the mother. Such a realization would help very much to minimize the conflict between the sexes.

Of course, that is not the only cause of the conflict. There is another, as expressed by *Laura:* "Do you remember when I first came into your life, I was like a second mother? . . . I loved you as my child. But . . . when the nature of your feelings changed and you appeared as my lover, I blushed, and your embraces were joy that was followed by remorseful conscience as if my blood were ashamed."

The vile thought instilled into woman by the Church and Puritanism that sex expression without the purpose of procreation is immoral, has been a most degrading influence. It has poisoned the life of thousands of women who similarly suffer "remorseful conscience"; therefore their disgust and hatred of the man; therefore also the conflict.

Must it always be thus? Even Strindberg does not think so. Else he would not plead in behalf of "divorce between man and wife, so that lovers may be born." He felt that until man and woman cease to have "remorseful consciences" because of the most elemental expression of the joy of life, they cannot realize the purity and beauty of sex, nor appreciate its ecstasy, as the source of full understanding and creative harmony between male and female. Till then man and woman must remain in conflict, and the child pay the penalty.

August Strindberg, as one of the numberless innocent victims of this terrible conflict, cries out bitterly against it, with the artistic genius and strength that compel attention to the significance of his message.

MISS JULIE

In his masterly preface to this play, August Strindberg writes: "The fact that my tragedy makes a sad impression on many is the fault of the many. When we become strong, as were the first French revolutionaries, it will make an exclusively pleasant and cheerful impression to see the royal parks cleared of rotting, superannuated trees which have too long stood in the way of others with equal right to vegetate their full lifetime; it will make a good impression in the same sense as does the sight of the death of an incurable."

What a wealth of revolutionary thought,—were we to realize that those who will clear society of the rotting, superannuated trees that have so long been standing in the way of others entitled to an equal share in life, must be as strong as the great revolutionists of the past!

Indeed, Strindberg is no trimmer, no cheap reformer, no patchworker; therefore his inability to remain fixed, or to content himself with accepted truths. Therefore also, his great versatility, his deep grasp of the subtlest phases of life. Was he not forever the seeker, the restless spirit roaming the earth, ever in the death-throes of the Old, to give birth to the New? How, then, could he be other than relentless and grim and brutally frank.

"Miss Julie," a one-act tragedy, is no doubt a brutally frank portrayal of the most intimate thoughts of man and of the age-long antagonism between classes. Brutally frank, because August Strindberg strips both of their glitter, their sham and pretense, that we may see that "at bottom there's not so much difference between people and—people."

Who in modern dramatic art is there to teach us that lesson with the insight of an August Strindberg? He who had been tossed about all his life between the decadent traditions of his aristocratic father and the grim, sordid reality of the class of his mother. He who had been begotten through the physical mastery of his father and the physical subserviency of his mother. Verily, Strindberg knew whereof he spoke—for he spoke with his soul, a language whose significance is illuminating, compelling.

Miss Julie inherited the primitive, intense passion of her mother and the neurotic aristocratic tendencies of her father. Added to this heritage is the call of the wild, the "intense summer heat when the blood turns to fire, and when all are in a holiday spirit, full of gladness, and rank is flung aside." *Miss Julie* feels, when too late, that the barrier of rank reared through the ages, by wealth and power, is not flung aside with impunity. Therein the vicious brutality, the boundless injustice of rank.

The people on the estate of *Julie's* father are celebrating St. John's Eve with dance, song and revelry. The Count is absent, and *Julie* graciously mingles with the servants. But once having tasted the simple abandon of the people, once having thrown off the artifice and superficiality of her aristocratic decorum, her suppressed passions leap into full flame, and *Julie* throws herself into the arms of her father's valet, *Jean*—not because of love for the man, nor yet openly and freely, but as persons of her station may do when carried away by the moment.

The woman in *Julie* pursues the male, follows him into the kitchen, plays with him as with a pet dog, and then feigns indignation when *Jean*, aroused, makes advances. How dare he, the servant, the lackey, even insinuate that she would have him! "I, the lady of the house! I honor the people with my presence. I, in love with my coachman? I, who step down."

How well Strindberg knows the psychology of the upper classes! How well he understands that their graciousness, their charity, their interest in the "common people" is, after all, nothing but arrogance, blind conceit of their own importance and ignorance of the character of the people.

Even though *Jean* is a servant, he has his pride, he has his dreams. "I was not hired to be your plaything," he says to *Julie;* "I think too much of myself for that."

Strange, is it not, that those who serve and drudge for others, should think so much of themselves as to refuse to be played with? Stranger still that they should indulge in dreams. *Jean* says:

> Do you know how people in high life look from the under-world? . . . They look like hawks and eagles whose backs one seldom sees, for they soar up above. I lived in a hovel provided by the State, with seven brothers and sisters and a pig; out on a barren stretch where nothing grew, not even a tree, but from the window I could see the Count's park walls with apple trees rising above them. That was the garden of paradise; and there stood many angry angels with flaming swords protecting it; but for all that I and other boys found the way to the tree of life—now you despise me. . . . I thought if it is true that the thief on the cross could enter heaven and dwell among the angels it was strange that a pauper child on God's earth could not go into the castle park and play with the Countess' daughter. . . . What I wanted—I don't know. You were unattainable, but through the vision of you I was made to realize how hopeless it was to rise above the conditions of my birth.

What rich food for thought in the above for all of us, and for the Jeans, the people who do not know what they want, yet feel the cruelty of a world that keeps the pauper's child out of the castle of his dreams, away from joy and play and beauty! The injustice and the bitterness of it all, that places the stigma of birth as an impassable obstacle, a fatal imperative excluding one from the table of life, with the result of producing such terrible effects on the Julies and the Jeans. The one unnerved, made helpless and useless by affluence, ease and idleness; the other enslaved and bound by service and dependence. Even when *Jean* wants to, he cannot rise above his condition. When *Julie* asks him to embrace her, to love her, he replies:

> I can't as long as we are in this house. . . . There is the Count, your father. . . . I need only to see his gloves lying in a chair to feel my own insignificance. I have only to hear his bell, to start like a nervous horse. . . . And now that I see his boots standing there so stiff and proper, I feel like bowing and scraping. . . . I can't account for it but—but ah, it is that damned servant in my back—I believe if the Count came here now, and told me to cut my throat, I would

do it on the spot. . . . Superstition and prejudice taught in childhood can't be uprooted in a moment.

No, superstition and prejudice cannot be uprooted in a moment; nor in years. The awe of authority, servility before station and wealth—these are the curse of the Jean class that makes such cringing slaves of them. Cringing before those who are above them, tyrannical and overbearing toward those who are below them. For *Jean* has the potentiality of the master in him as much as that of the slave. Yet degrading as "the damned servant" reacts upon *Jean*, it is much more terrible in its effect upon *Kristin*, the cook, the dull, dumb animal who has so little left of the spirit of independence that she has lost even the ambition to rise above her condition. Thus when *Kristin*, the betrothed of Jean, discovers that her mistress *Julie* had given herself to him, she is indignant that her lady should have so much forgotten her station as to stoop to her father's valet.

Kristin. I don't want to be here in this house any longer where one cannot respect one's betters.

Jean. Why should one respect them?

Kristin. Yes, you can say that, you are so smart. But I don't want to serve people who behave so. It reflects on oneself, I think.

Jean. Yes, but it's a comfort that they're not a bit better than we.

Kristin. No, I don't think so, for if they are not better there's no use in our trying to better ourselves in this world. And to think of the Count! Think of him who has had so much sorrow all his days. No, I don't want to stay in this house any longer! And to think of it being with such as you! If it had been the Lieutenant— . . . I have never lowered my position. Let any one say, if they can, that the Count's cook has had anything to do with the riding master or the swineherd. Let them come and say it!

Such dignity and morality are indeed pathetic, because they indicate how completely serfdom may annihilate even the longing for something higher and better in the breast of a human being. The Kristins represent the greatest obstacle to social growth, the deadlock in the conflict between the classes. On the other hand, the Jeans, with all their longing for higher possibilities, often become brutalized in the hard school of life; though in the conflict with *Julie*, *Jean* shows brutality only at the critical moment, when it becomes a question of life and death, a moment that means discovery and consequent ruin, or safety for both.

Jean, though the male is aroused in him, pleads with *Julie* not to play with fire, begs her to return to her room, and not to give the servants a chance for gossip. And when later *Jean* suggests his room for a hiding place that *Julie* may escape the approaching merry-makers, it is to save her from their songs full of insinuation and ribaldry. Finally when the inevitable happens, when as a result of their closeness in *Jean's* room, of their overwrought nerves, their intense passion, the avalanche of sex sweeps them off their feet, forgetful of station, birth and conventions, and they return to the kitchen, it is again *Jean* who is willing to bear his share of the responsibility. "I don't care to shirk my share of the blame," he tells *Julie,* "but do you think any one of my position would have dared to raise his eyes to you if you had not invited it?"

There is more truth in this statement than the Julies can grasp, namely, that even servants have their passions and feelings that cannot long be trifled with, with impunity. The Jeans know "that it is the glitter of brass, not gold, that dazzles us from below, and that the eagle's back is gray like the rest of him." For *Jean* says, "I'm sorry to have to realize that all that I have looked up to is not worth while, and it pains me to see you fallen lower than your cook, as it pains me to see autumn blossoms whipped to pieces by the cold rain and transformed into—dirt!"

It is this force that helps to transform the blossom into dirt that August Strindberg emphasizes in "The Father." For the child born against the will of its parents must also be without will, and too weak to bear the stress and storm of life. In "Miss Julie" this idea recurs with even more tragic effect. *Julie,* too, had been brought into the world against her mother's wishes. Indeed, so much did her mother dread the thought of a child that she "was always ill, she often had cramps and acted queerly, often hiding in the orchard or the attic." Added to this horror was the conflict, the relentless war of traditions between *Julie's* aristocratic father and her mother descended from the people. This was the heritage of the innocent victim, *Julie*—an autumn blossom blown into fragments by lack of stability, lack of love and lack of harmony. In other words, while *Julie* is broken and weakened by her inheritance and environment, *Jean* is hardened by his.

When *Jean* kills the bird which *Julie* wants to rescue from the ruins of her life, it is not so much out of real cruelty, as it is because the character of *Jean* was molded in the relentless school of necessity, in which only those survive who have the determination to act in time of danger. For as *Jean* says, "Miss Julie, I see that you are unhappy, I know that you are suffering, but I cannot understand you. Among my kind there is no nonsense of this sort. We love as we play—when work gives us time. We haven't the whole day and night for it as you."

Here we have the key to the psychology of the utter helplessness and weakness of the Julie type, and of the brutality of the Jeans. The one, the result of an empty life, of parasitic leisure, of a useless, purposeless existence. The other, the effect of too little time for development, for maturity and depth; of too much toil to permit the growth of the finer traits in the human soul.

August Strindberg, himself the result of the class conflict between his parents, never felt at home with either of them. All his life he was galled by the irreconcilability of the classes; and though he was no sermonizer in the sense of offering a definite panacea for individual or social ills, yet with master touch he painted the degrading effects of class distinction and its tragic antagonisms. In "Miss Julie" he popularized one of the most vital problems of our age, and gave to the world a work powerful in its grasp of elemental emotions, laying bare the human soul behind the mask of social tradition and class culture.

COMRADES

Although "Comrades" was written in 1888, it is in a measure the most up-to-date play of Strindberg,—so thoroughly modern that one at all conversant with the *milieu* that inspired "Comrades" could easily point out the type of character portrayed in the play.

It is a four-act comedy of marriage—the kind of marriage that lacks social and legal security in the form of a ceremony, but retains all the petty conventions of the marriage institution. The results of such an anomaly are indeed ludicrous when viewed from a distance, but very tragic for those who play a part in it.

Axel Alberg and his wife *Bertha* are Swedish artists residing in Paris. They are both painters. Of course they share the same living quarters, and although each has a separate room, the arrangement does not hinder them from trying to regulate each other's movements. Thus when *Bertha* does not arrive on time to keep her engagement with her model, *Axel* is provoked; and when he takes the liberty to chide her for her tardiness, his wife is indignant at the "invasiveness" of her husband, because women of the type of *Bertha* are as sensitive to fair criticism as their ultra-conservative sisters. Nor is *Bertha* different in her concept of love, which is expressed in the following dialogue:

Bertha. Will you be very good, very, very good?
Axel. I always want to be good to you, my friend.

Bertha, who has sent her painting to the exhibition, wants to make use of *Axel's* "goodness" to secure the grace of one of the art jurors.

Bertha. You would not make a sacrifice for your wife, would you?
Axel. Go begging? No, I don't want to do that.

Bertha immediately concludes that he does not love her and that, more-over, he is jealous of her art. There is a scene.
Bertha soon recovers. But bent on gaining her purpose, she changes her manner.

Bertha. Axel, let's be friends! And hear me a moment. Do you think that my position in your house—for it is yours—is agreeable to me? You support me, you pay for my studying at Julian's, while you yourself cannot afford instruction. Don't you think I see how you sit and wear out yourself and your talent on these pot-boiling drawings, and are able to paint only in leisure moments? You haven't been able to afford models for yourself, while you pay mine five hard-earned francs an hour. You don't know how good—how noble—how sacrificing you are, and also you don't know how I suffer to see you toil so for me. Oh, Axel, you can't know how I feel my position. What am I to you? Of what use am I in your house? Oh, I blush when I think about it!
Axel. What talk! Isn't a man to support his wife?
Bertha. I don't want it. And you, Axel, you must help me. I'm not your equal when it's like that, but I could be if you would humble yourself once, just once! Don't think that you are alone in going to one of the jury to say a good word for another. If it were for yourself, it would be another matter, but for me—Forgive me! Now I beg of you as nicely as I know how. Lift me from my humiliating position to your side, and I'll be so grateful I shall never trouble you again with reminding you of my position. Never, Axel!

Yet though *Bertha* gracefully accepts everything *Axel* does for her, with as little compunction as the ordinary wife, she does not give as much in return as the latter. On the contrary, she exploits *Axel* in a thousand ways, squanders his hard-earned money, and lives the life of the typical wifely parasite. August Strindberg could not help attacking with much bitterness such a farce and outrage parading in the disguise of radicalism. For *Bertha* is not an exceptional, isolated case. To-day, as when Strindberg satirized the all-too-feminine, the majority of so-called emancipated women are willing to accept, like *Bertha,* everything from the man, and yet feel highly indignant if he asks in return the simple comforts of married life. The ordinary wife, at least, does not pretend to play an important rôle in the life of her husband. But the Berthas deceive themselves and others with the notion that the "emancipated" wife is a great moral force, an inspiration to the man. Whereas in reality she is often a cold-blooded exploiter of the work and ideas of the man, a heavy handicap to his life-purpose, retarding his growth as effectively as did her grandmothers in the long ago. *Bertha* takes advantage of *Axel's* affection to further her own artistic ambitions, just as the Church and State married woman uses her husband's love to advance her social ambitions. It never occurs to *Bertha* that she is no less despicable than her legally married sister. She cannot understand *Axel's* opposition to an art that clamors only for approval, distinction and decorations.

However, *Axel* can not resist *Bertha's* pleadings. He visits the patron saint of the salon, who, by the way, is not M. Roubey, but Mme. Roubey; for she is the "President of the Woman-Painter Protective Society." What chance would *Bertha* have with one of her own sex in authority? Hence her husband must be victimized. During *Axel's* absence *Bertha* learns that his picture has been refused by the salon, while hers is accepted. She is not in the least disturbed, nor at all concerned over the effect of the news on *Axel.* On the contrary, she is rather pleased because "so many women are refused that a man might put up with it, and be made to feel it once."

In her triumph *Bertha's* attitude to *Axel* becomes overbearing; she humiliates him, belittles his art, and even plans to humble him before the guests invited to celebrate *Bertha's* artistic success.

But *Axel* is tearing himself free from the meshes of his decaying love. He begins to see *Bertha* as she is: her unscrupulousness in money matters, her ceaseless effort to emasculate him. In a terrible word tussle he tells her: "I had once been free, but you clipped the hair of my strength while my tired head lay in your lap. During sleep you stole my best blood."

In the last act *Bertha* discovers that *Axel* had generously changed the numbers on the paintings in order to give her a better chance. It was *his* picture that was chosen as *her* work. She feels ashamed and humiliated; but it is too late. *Axel* leaves her with the exclamation, "I want to meet my comrades in the café, but at home I want a wife."

A characteristic sidelight in the play is given by the conversation of *Mrs. Hall,* the divorced wife of *Doctor Ostermark.* She comes to Bertha with a bitter tirade against the Doctor because he gives her insufficient alimony.

Mrs. Hall. And now that the girls are grown up and about to start in life, now he writes us that he is bankrupt and that he can't send us more than half the allowance. Isn't that nice, just now when the girls are grown up and are going out into life?

Bertha. We must look into this. He'll be here in a few days. Do you know that you have the law on your side and that the courts can force him to pay? And he shall be forced to do so. Do you understand? So, he can bring children into the world and then leave them empty-handed with the poor deserted mother.

Bertha, who believes in woman's equality with man, and in her economic independence, yet delivers herself of the old sentimental gush in behalf of "the poor deserted mother," who has been supported by her husband for years, though their relations had ceased long before.

A distorted picture, some feminists will say. Not at all. It is as typical to-day as it was twenty-six years ago. Even to-day some "emancipated" women claim the right to be self-supporting, yet demand their husband's support. In fact, many leaders in the American suffrage movement assure us that when women will make laws, they will force men to support their wives. From the leaders down to the simplest devotee, the same attitude prevails, namely, that man is a *blagueur,* and that but for him the Berthas would have long ago become Michelangelos, Beethovens, or Shakespeares; they claim that the Berthas represent the most virtuous half of the race, and that they have made up their minds to make man as virtuous as they are.

That such ridiculous extravagance should be resented by the Axels is not at all surprising. It is resented even by the more intelligent of *Bertha's* own sex. Not because they are opposed to the emancipation of woman, but because they do not believe that her emancipation can ever be achieved by such absurd and hysterical notions. They repudiate the idea that people who retain the substance of their slavery and merely escape the shadow, can possibly be free, live free, or act free.

The radicals, no less than the feminists, must realize that a mere external change in their economic and political status, cannot alter the inherent or acquired prejudices and superstitions which underlie their slavery and dependence, and which are the main causes of the antagonism between the sexes.

The transition period is indeed a most difficult and perilous stage for the woman as well as for the man. It requires a powerful light to guide us past the dangerous reefs and rocks in the ocean of life. August Strindberg is such a light. Sometimes glaring, ofttimes scorching, but always beneficially illuminating the path for those who walk in darkness, for the blind ones who would rather deceive and be deceived than look into the recesses of their being. Therefore August Strindberg is not only "the spiritual conscience of Sweden," as he has been called, but the spiritual conscience of the whole human family, and, as such, a most vital revolutionary factor.

THE GERMAN DRAMA

HERMANN SUDERMANN

It has been said that military conquest generally goes hand in hand with the decline of creative genius, with the retrogression of culture. I believe this is not a mere assertion. The history of the human race repeatedly demonstrates that whenever a nation achieved great military success, it invariably involved the decline of art, of literature, of the drama; in short, of culture in the deepest and finest sense. This has been particularly borne out by Germany after its military triumph in the Franco-Prussian War.

For almost twenty years after that war, the country of poets and thinkers remained, intellectually, a veritable desert, barren of ideas. Young Germany had to go for its intellectual food to France,—Daudet, Maupassant, and Zola; or to Russia—Tolstoy, Turgenev, and Dostoyevski; finally also to Ibsen and Strindberg. Nothing thrived in Germany during that period, except a sickening patriotism and sentimental romanticism, perniciously misleading the people and giving them no adequate outlook upon life and the social struggle. Perhaps that accounts for the popular vogue of Hermann Sudermann: it may explain why he was received by the young generation with open arms and acclaimed a great artist.

It is not my intention to discuss Hermann Sudermann as an artist or to consider him from the point of view of the technique of the drama. I intend to deal with him as the first German dramatist to treat social topics and discuss the pressing questions of the day. From this point of view Hermann Sudermann may be regarded as the pioneer of a new era in the German drama. Primarily is this true of the three plays "Honor," "Magda," and "The Fires of St. John." In these dramas Hermann Sudermann, while not delving deeply into the causes of the social conflicts, nevertheless touches upon many vital subjects.

In "Honor" the author demolishes the superficial, sentimental conception of "honor" that is a purely external manifestation, having no roots in the life, the habits, or the customs of the people. He exposes the stupidity of the notion that because a man looks askance at you, or fails to pay respect to your uniform, you must challenge him to a duel and shoot him dead. In this play Sudermann shows that the conception of honor is nothing fixed or permanent, but that it varies with economic and social status, different races, peoples and times holding different ideas of it. With "Honor" Sudermann succeeded in undermining to a considerable extent the stupid and ridiculous notion of the Germans ruled by the rod and the Kaiser's coat.

But I particularly wish to consider "Magda," because, of all the plays written by Hermann Sudermann, it is the most revolutionary and the least national. It deals with a universal subject,—the awakening of woman. It is revolutionary, not because Sudermann was the first to treat this subject, for Ibsen had preceded him, but because in "Magda" he was the first to raise the question of woman's right to motherhood with or without the sanction of State and Church.

MAGDA

Lieutenant Colonel Schwartze, *Magda's* father, represents all the conventional and conservative notions of society.

Schwartze. Modern ideas! Oh, pshaw! I know them. But come into the quiet homes where are bred brave soldiers and virtuous wives. There you'll hear no talk about heredity, no arguments about individuality, no scandalous gossip. There modern ideas have no foothold, for it is there that the life and strength of the Fatherland abide. Look at this home! There is no luxury, —hardly even what you call good taste,—faded rugs, birchen chairs, old pictures; and yet when you see the beams of the western sun pour through the white curtains and lie with such a loving touch on the old room, does not something say to you, "Here dwells true happiness"?

The *Colonel* is a rigid military man. He is utterly blind to the modern conception of woman's place in life. He rules his family as the Kaiser rules the nation, with severe discipline, with terrorism and despotism. He chooses the man whom *Magda* is to marry, and when she refuses to accept his choice, he drives her out of the house.

At the age of eighteen *Magda* goes out into the world yearning for development; she longs for artistic expression and economic independence. Seventeen years later she returns to her native town, a celebrated singer. As

Madelene dell' Orto she is invited to sing at the town's charity bazaar, and is acclaimed, after the performance, one of the greatest stars of the country.

Magda has not forgotten her home; especially does she long to see her father whom she loves passionately, and her sister, whom she had left a little child of eight. After the concert *Magda,* the renowned artist, steals away from her admirers, with their flowers and presents, and goes out into the darkness of the night to catch a glimpse, through the window at least, of her father and her little sister.

Magda's father is scandalized at her mode of life: what will people say if the daughter of the distinguished officer stops at a hotel, associates with men without a chaperon, and is wined and dined away from her home? *Magda* is finally prevailed upon to remain with her parents. She consents on condition that they should not pry into her life, that they should not soil and besmirch her innermost being. But that is expecting the impossible from a provincial environment. It is not that her people really question; but they insinuate, they speak with looks and nods; burning curiosity to unearth *Magda's* life in the very air.

Schwartze. I implore you—Come here, my child—nearer—so—I implore you—let me be happy in my dying hour. Tell me that you have remained pure in body and soul, and then go with my blessing on your way.

Magda. I have remained—true to myself, dear father.

Schwartze. How? In good or in ill?

Magda. In what—for me—was good.

Schwartze. I love you with my whole heart, because I have sorrowed for you—so long. But I must know who you are.

Among the townspeople who come to pay homage to *Magda* is *Councillor von Keller.* In his student days he belonged to the bohemian set and was full of advanced ideas. At that period he met *Magda,* young, beautiful, and inexperienced. A love affair developed. But when *Von Keller* finished his studies, he went home to the fold of his family, and forgot his sweetheart *Magda.* In due course he became an important pillar of society, a very influential citizen, admired, respected, and feared in the community.

When *Magda* returns home, *Von Keller* comes to pay her his respects. But she is no longer the insignificant little girl he had known; she is now a celebrity. What pillar of society is averse to basking in the glow of celebrities? *Von Keller* offers flowers and admiration. But *Magda* discovers in him the man who had robbed her of her faith and trust,—the father of her child. *Magda* has become purified by her bitter struggle. It made her finer and bigger. She does not even reproach the man, because—

Magda. I've painted this meeting to myself a thousand times, and have been prepared for it for years. Something warned me, too, when I undertook this journey home—though I must say I hardly expected just here to—Yes, how is it that, after what has passed between us, you came into this house? It seems to me a little— . . . I can see it all. The effort to keep worthy of respect under such difficulties, with a bad conscience, is awkward. You look down from the height of your pure atmosphere on your sinful youth,—for you are called a pillar, my dear friend.

Von Keller. Well, I felt myself called to higher things. I thought—Why should I undervalue my position? I have become Councillor, and that comparatively young. An ordinary ambition might take satisfaction in that. But one sits and waits at home, while others are called to the ministry. And this environment, conventionality, and narrowness, all is so gray,—gray! And the ladies here—for one who cares at all about elegance—I assure you something rejoiced within me when I read this morning that you were the famous singer,—you to whom I was tied by so many dear memories and—

Magda. And then you thought whether it might not be possible with the help of these dear memories to bring a little color into the gray background?

Von Keller. Oh, pray don't—

Magda. Well, between old friends—

Von Keller. Really, are we that, really?

Magda. Certainly, *sans rancune.* Oh, if I took it from the other standpoint, I should have to range the whole gamut,—liar, coward, traitor! But as I look at it, I owe you nothing but thanks, my friend.

Von Keller. This is a view which—

Magda. Which is very convenient for you. But why should I not make it convenient for you? In the manner in which we met, you had no obligations towards me. I had left my home; I was young and innocent, hot-blooded and careless, and I lived as I saw others live. I gave myself to you because I loved you. I might perhaps have loved anyone who came in my way. That—that seemed to be all over. And we were so happy,—weren't we? . . . Yes, we were a merry set; and when the fun had lasted half a year, one day my lover vanished.

Von Keller. An unlucky chance, I swear to you. My father was ill. I had to travel. I wrote everything to you.

Magda. H'm! I didn't reproach you. And now I will tell you why I owe you thanks. I was a stupid, unsuspecting thing, enjoying freedom like a runaway monkey. Through you I became a woman. For whatever I have done in my art, for whatever I have become in myself, I have you to thank. My soul was like—yes, down below there, there used to be an Æolian harp which was left moldering because my father could not bear it. Such a silent harp was my soul; and through you it was given to the storm. And it sounded almost to breaking,—the whole scale of passions which bring us women to maturity,—love and hate and revenge and ambition, and need, need, need,—three times need—and the highest, the strongest, the holiest of all, the mother's love!—All I owe to you!

Von Keller. My child!

Magda. Your child? Who calls it so? Yours? Ha, ha! Dare to claim portion in him and I'll kill you with these hands. Who are you? You're a strange man who gratified his lust and passed on with a laugh. But I have a child,—my son, my God, my all! For him I lived and starved and froze and walked the streets; for him I sang and danced in concert-halls,—for my child who was crying for his bread!

Von Keller. For Heaven's sake, hush! someone's coming.

Magda. Let them come! Let them all come! I don't care, I don't care! To their faces I'll say what I think of you,—of you and your respectable society. Why should I be worse than you, that I must prolong my existence among you by a lie! Why should this gold upon my body, and the lustre which surrounds my name, only increase my infamy? Have I not worked early and late for ten long years? Have I not woven this dress with sleepless nights? Have I not built up my career step by step, like thousands of my kind? Why should I blush before anyone? I am myself, and through myself I have become what I am.

Magda's father learns about the affair and immediately demands that the *Councillor* marry his daughter, or fight a duel. *Magda* resents the preposterous idea. *Von Keller* is indeed glad to offer *Magda* his hand in marriage: she is so beautiful and fascinating; she will prove a great asset to his ambitions. But he stipulates that she give up her profession of singer, and that the existence of the child be kept secret. He tells *Magda* that later on, when they are happily married and firmly established in the world, they will bring their child to their home and adopt it; but for the present respectability must not know that it is theirs, born out of wedlock, without the sanction of the Church and the State.

That is more than *Magda* can endure. She is outraged that she, the mother, who had given up everything for the sake of her child, who had slaved, struggled and drudged in order to win a career and economic independence—all for the sake of the child—that she should forswear her right to motherhood, her right to be true to herself!

Magda. What—what do you say?

Von Keller. Why, it would ruin us. No, no, it is absurd to think of it. But we can make a little journey every year to wherever it is being educated. One can register under a false name; that is not unusual in foreign parts, and is hardly criminal. And when we are fifty years old, and other regular conditions have been fulfilled, that can be arranged, can't it? Then we can, under some pretext, adopt it, can't we?

Magda. I have humbled myself, I have surrendered my judgment, I have let myself be carried like a lamb to the slaughter. But my child I will not leave. Give up my child to save his career!

Magda orders *Von Keller* out of the house. But the old *Colonel* is unbending. He insists that his daughter become an honorable woman by marrying the man who had seduced her. Her refusal fires his wrath to wild rage.

Schwartze. Either you swear to me now . . . that you will become the honorable wife of your child's father, or—neither of us two shall go out of this room alive. . . . You think . . . because you are free and a great artist, that you can set at naught—

Magda. Leave art out of the question. Consider me nothing more than the seamstress or the servant-maid who seeks, among strangers, the little food and the little love she needs. See how much the family with its morality demand from us! It throws us on our own resources, it gives us neither shelter nor happiness, and yet, in our loneliness, we must live according to the laws which it has planned for itself alone. We must still crouch in the corner, and there wait patiently until a respectful wooer happens to come. Yes, wait. And meanwhile the war for existence of body and soul is consuming us. Ahead we see nothing but sorrow and despair, and yet shall we not once dare to give what we have of youth and strength to the man for whom our whole being cries? Gag us, stupefy us, shut us up in harems or in cloisters—and that perhaps would be best. But if you give us our freedom, do not wonder if we take advantage of it.

But morality and the family never understand the Magdas. Least of all does the old Colonel understand his daughter. Rigid in his false notions and superstitions, wrought up with distress, he is about to carry out his threat, when a stroke of apoplexy overtakes him.

In "Magda," Hermann Sudermann has given to the world a new picture of modern womanhood, a type of free motherhood. As such the play is of great revolutionary significance, not alone to Germany, but to the universal spirit of a newer day.

THE FIRES OF ST. JOHN

In "The Fires of St. John," Sudermann does not go as far as in "Magda." Nevertheless the play deals with important truths. Life does not always draw the same conclusions; life is not always logical, not always consistent. The function of the artist is to portray Life—only thus can he be true both to art and to life.

In this drama we witness the bondage of gratitude,—one of the most enslaving and paralyzing factors. *Mr. Brauer,* a landed proprietor, has a child, *Gertrude,* a beautiful girl, who has always lived the sheltered life of a hothouse plant. The Brauers also have an adopted daughter, *Marie,* whom they had picked up on the road, while traveling on a stormy night. They called her "the calamity child," because a great misfortune had befallen them shortly before. *Mr. Brauer's* younger brother, confronted with heavy losses, had shot himself, leaving behind his son *George* and a heavily mortgaged estate. The finding of the baby, under these circumstances, was considered by the Brauers an omen. They adopted it and brought it up as their own.

This involved the forcible separation of *Marie* from her gypsy mother, who was a pariah, an outcast beggar. She drank and stole in order to subsist. But with it all, her mother instinct was strong and it always drove her back to the place where her child lived. *Marie* had her first shock when, on her way home from confirmation, the ragged and brutalized woman threw herself before the young girl, crying, "Mamie, my child, my Mamie!" It was then that *Marie* realized her origin. Out of gratitude she consecrated her life to the Brauers.

Marie never forgot for a moment that she owed everything—her education, her support and happiness—to her adopted parents. She wrapped herself around them with all the intensity and passion of her nature. She became the very spirit of the house. She looked after the estate, and devoted herself to little *Gertrude,* as to her own sister.

Gertrude is engaged to marry her cousin *George,* and everything is beautiful and joyous in the household. No one suspects that *Marie* has been in love with the young man ever since her childhood. However, because of her gratitude to her benefactors, she stifles her nature, hardens her heart, and locks her feelings behind closed doors, as it were. And when *Gertrude* is about to marry *George, Marie* throws herself into the work of fixing up a home for the young people, to surround them with sunshine and joy in their new love life.

Accidentally *Marie* discovers a manuscript written by *George,* wherein he discloses his deep love for her. She learns that he, even as she, has no other thought, no other purpose in life than his love for her. But he is also bound by gratitude for his uncle *Brauer* who had saved the honor of his father and had rescued him from poverty. He feels it dishonorable to refuse to marry *Gertrude.*

George. All these years I have struggled and deprived myself with only one thing in view—to be free—free—and yet I must bow—I must bow. If it were not for the sake of this beautiful child, who is innocent of it all, I would be tempted to—But the die is cast, the yoke is ready—and so am I! . . . I, too, am a child of misery, a calamity child; but I am a subject of charity. I accept all they have to give . . . Was I not picked up from the street, as my uncle so kindly informed me for the second time—like yourself? Do I not belong to this house, and am I not smothered with the damnable charity of my benefactors, like yourself?

It is St. John's night. The entire family is gathered on the estate of the Brauers, while the peasants are making merry with song and dance at the lighted bonfires.

It is a glorious, dreamy night, suggestive of symbolic meaning. According to the servant *Katie,* it is written that "whoever shall give or receive their first kiss on St. John's eve, their love is sealed and they will be faithful unto death."

In the opinion of the *Pastor,* St. John's night represents a religious phase, too holy for flippant pagan joy.

Pastor. On such a dreamy night, different emotions are aroused within us. We seem to be able to look into the future, and imagine ourselves able to fathom all mystery and heal all wounds. The common becomes elevated, our wishes become fate; and now we ask ourselves: What is it that causes all this within us—all these desires and wishes? It is *love,* brotherly love, that has been planted in our souls, that fills our lives: and, it is life itself. Am I not right? And now, with one bound, I will come to the point. In the revelation you will find: "God is love." Yes, God is love; and that is the most beautiful trait of our religion—that the best, the most beautiful within us, has been granted us by Him above. Then how could I, this very evening, so overcome with feeling for my fellow-man—how could I pass Him by? Therefore, Mr. Brauer, no matter, whether pastor or layman, I must confess my inability to grant your wish, and decline to give you a genuine pagan toast—

But Christian symbolism having mostly descended from primitive pagan custom, *George's* view is perhaps the most significant.

George. Since the Pastor has so eloquently withdrawn, I will give you a toast. For, you see, my dear Pastor, something of the old pagan, a spark of heathenism, is still glowing somewhere within us all. It has outlived century after century, from the time of the old Teutons. Once every year that spark is fanned into flame—it flames up high, and then it is called "The Fires of St. John." Once every year we have "free night." Then the witches ride upon their brooms—the same brooms with which their witchcraft was once driven out of them—with scornful laughter the wild hordes sweep across the tree-tops, up, up, high upon the Blocksberg! Then it is, when in our hearts awake those wild desires which our fates could not fulfill—and, understand me well, dared not fulfill—then, no matter what may be the name of the law that governs the world on that day, in order that one single wish may become a reality, by whose grace we prolong our miserable existence, thousand others must miserably perish, part because they were never attainable; but the others, yes, the others, because we allowed them to escape us like wild birds, which, though already in our hands, but too listless to profit by opportunity, we failed to grasp at the right moment. But no matter. Once every year we have "free night." And yonder tongues of fire shooting up towards the heavens—do you know what they are? They are the spirits of our dead perished wishes! That is the red plumage of our birds of paradise we might have petted and nursed through our entire lives, but have escaped us! That is the old chaos, the heathenism within us; and though we be happy in sunshine and according to law, to-night is St. John's night. To its ancient pagan fires I empty this glass. To-night they shall burn and flame up high—high and again high!

George and *Marie* meet. They, too, have had their instinct locked away even from their own consciousness. And on this night they break loose with tremendous, primitive force. They are driven into each other's arms because they feel that they belong to each other; they know that if they had the strength they could take each other by the hand, face their benefactor and tell him the truth: tell him that it would be an unpardonable crime for *George* to marry *Gertrude* when he loves another woman.

Now they all but find courage and strength for it, when the pitiful plaint reaches them, "Oh, mine Mamie, mine daughter, mine child." And *Marie* is cast down from the sublime height of her love and passion, down to the realization that she also, like her pariah mother, must go out into the world to struggle, to fight, to become free from the bondage of gratitude, of charity and dependence.

Not so *George*. He goes to the altar, like many another man, with a lie upon his lips. He goes to swear that all his life long he will love, protect and shelter the woman who is to be his wife.

This play is rich in thought and revolutionary significance. For is it not true that we are all bound by gratitude, tied and fettered by what we think we owe to others? Are we not thus turned into weaklings and cowards, and do we not enter into new relationships with lies upon our lips? Do we not become a lie to ourselves and a lie to those we associate with? And whether we have the strength to be true to the dominant spirit, warmed into being by the fires of St. John; whether we have the courage to live up to it always or whether it manifests itself only on occasion, it is nevertheless true that there is the potentiality of freedom in the soul of every man and every woman; that there is the possibility of greatness and fineness in all beings, were they not bound and gagged by gratitude, by duty and shams,—a vicious network that enmeshes body and soul.

GERHART HAUPTMANN

LONELY LIVES

GERHART HAUPTMANN is the dramatist of whom it may be justly said that he revolutionized the spirit of dramatic art in Germany: the last Mohican of a group of four—Ibsen, Strindberg, Tolstoy, and Hauptmann—who illumined the horizon of the nineteenth century. Of these Hauptmann, undoubtedly the most human, is also the most universal.

It is unnecessary to make comparisons between great artists: life is sufficiently complex to give each his place in the great scheme of things. If, then, I consider Hauptmann more human, it is because of his deep kinship with every stratum of life. While Ibsen deals exclusively with *one* attitude, Hauptmann embraces all, understands all, and portrays all, because nothing human is alien to him.

Whether it be the struggle of the transition stage in "Lonely Lives," or the conflict between the Ideal and the Real in "The Sunken Bell," or the brutal background of poverty in "The Weavers," Hauptmann is never aloof as the iconoclast Ibsen, never as bitter as the soul dissector Strindberg, nor yet as set as the crusader Tolstoy. And that because of his humanity, his boundless love, his oneness with the disinherited of the earth, and his sympathy with the struggles and the travail, the hope and the despair of every human soul. That accounts for the bitter opposition which met Gerhart Hauptmann when he made his first appearance as a dramatist; but it also accounts for the love and devotion of those to whom he was a battle cry, a clarion call against all iniquity, injustice and wrong.

In "Lonely Lives" we see the wonderful sympathy, the tenderness of Hauptmann permeating every figure of the drama.

Dr. Vockerat is not a fighter, not a propagandist or a soap-box orator; he is a dreamer, a poet, and above all a searcher for truth; a scientist, a man who lives in the realm of thought and ideas, and is out of touch with reality and his immediate surroundings.

His parents are simple folk, religious and devoted. To them the world is a book with seven seals. Having lived all their life on a farm, everything with them is regulated and classified into simple ideas—good or bad, great or small, strong or weak. How can they know the infinite shades between strong and weak, how could they grasp the endless variations between the good and the bad? To them life is a daily routine of work and prayer. God has arranged everything, and God manages everything. Why bother your head? Why spend sleepless nights? "Leave it all to God." What pathos in this childish simplicity!

They love their son *John,* they worship him, and they consecrate their lives to their only boy; and because of their love for him, also to his wife and the newly born baby. They have but one sorrow: their son has turned away from religion. Still greater their grief that *John* is an admirer of Darwin, Spencer and Haeckel and other such men,—sinners, heathens all, who will burn in purgatory and hell. To protect their beloved son from the punishment of God, the old folks continuously pray, and give still more devotion and love to their erring child.

Kitty, Dr. Vockerat's wife, is a beautiful type of the Gretchen, reared without any ideas about life, without any consciousness of her position in the world, a tender, helpless flower. She loves *John;* he is her ideal; he is her all. But she cannot understand him. She does not live in his sphere, nor speak his language. She has never dreamed his thoughts,—not because she is not willing or not eager to give the man all that he needs, but because she does not understand and does not know how.

Into this atmosphere comes *Anna Mahr* like a breeze from the plains. *Anna* is a Russian girl, a woman so far produced in Russia only, perhaps because the conditions, the life struggles of that country have been such as to develop a different type of woman. *Anna Mahr* has spent most of her life on the firing line. She has no conception of the personal: she is universal in her feelings and thoughts, with deep sympathies going out in abundance to all mankind.

When she comes to the Vockerats, their whole life is disturbed, especially that of *John Vockerat,* to whom she is like a balmy spring to the parched wanderer in the desert. She understands him, for has she not dreamed such thoughts as his, associated with men and women who, for the sake of the ideal, sacrificed their lives, went to Siberia, and suffered in the underground dungeons? How then could she fail a Vockerat? It is quite natural that *John* should find in *Anna* what his own little world could not give him,— understanding, comradeship, deep spiritual kinship.

The Anna Mahrs give the same to any one, be it man, woman or child. For theirs is not a feeling of sex, of the personal; it is the selfless, the human, the all-embracing fellowship.

In the invigorating presence of *Anna Mahr, John Vockerat* begins to live, to dream and work. Another phase of him, as it were, comes into being; larger vistas open before his eyes, and his life is filled with new aspiration for creative work in behalf of a liberating purpose.

Alas, the inevitability that the ideal should be besmirched and desecrated when it comes in contact with sordid reality! This tragic fate befalls *Anna Mahr* and *John Vockerat.*

Old *Mother Vockerat,* who, in her simplicity of soul cannot conceive of an intimate friendship between a man and a woman, unless they be husband and wife, begins first to suspect and insinuate, then to nag and interfere. Of course, it is her love for *John,* and even more so her love for her son's wife, who is suffering in silence and wearing out her soul in her realization of how little she can mean to her husband.

Mother Vockerat interprets *Kitty's* grief in a different manner: jealousy, and antagonism to the successful rival is her most convenient explanation for the loneliness, the heart-hunger of love. But as a matter of fact, it is something deeper and more vital that is born in *Kitty's* soul. It is the awakening of her own womanhood, of her personality.

Kitty. I agree with Miss Mahr on many points. She was saying lately that we women live in a condition of degradation. I think she is quite right there. It is what I feel very often. . . . It's as clear as daylight that she is right. We are really and truly a despised and ill-used sex. Only think that there is still a law—so she told me yesterday—which allows the husband to inflict a moderate amount of corporal punishment on his wife.

And yet, corporal punishment is not half as terrible as the punishment society inflicts on the Kittys by rearing them as dependent and useless beings, as hot-house flowers, ornaments for a fine house, but of no substance to the husband and certainly of less to her children.

And *Mother Vockerat,* without any viciousness, instills poison into the innocent soul of *Kitty* and embitters the life of her loved son. Ignorantly, *Mother Vockerat* meddles, interferes, and tramples upon the most sacred feelings, the innocent joys of true comradeship.

And all the time *John* and *Anna* are quite unaware of the pain and tragedy they are the cause of: they are far removed from the commonplace, petty world about them. They walk and discuss, read and argue about the wonders of life, the needs of humanity, the beauty of the ideal. They have both been famished so long: *John* for spiritual communion, *Anna* for warmth of home that she had known so little before, and which in her simplicity she has accepted at the hand of *Mother Vockerat* and *Kitty,* oblivious of the fact that nothing is so enslaving as hospitality prompted by a sense of duty.

Miss Mahr. It is a great age that we live in. That which has so weighed upon people's minds and darkened their lives seems to me to be gradually disappearing. Do you not think so, Dr. Vockerat?

John. How do you mean?

Miss Mahr. On the one hand we were oppressed by a sense of uncertainty, of apprehension, on the other by gloomy fanaticism. This exaggerated tension is calming down, is yielding to the influence of something like a current of fresh air, that is blowing in upon us from—let us say from the twentieth century.

John. But I don't find it possible to arrive at any real joy in life yet. I don't know. . . .

Miss Mahr. It has no connection with our individual fates—our little fates, Dr. Vockerat! . . . I have something to say to you—but you are not to get angry; you are to be quite quiet and good. . . . Dr. Vockerat! we also are falling into the error of weak natures. We must look at things more impersonally. We must learn to take ourselves less seriously.

John. But we'll not talk about that at present. . . . And is one really to sacrifice everything that one has gained to this cursed conventionality? Are people incapable of understanding that there can be no crime in a situation which only tends to make both parties better and nobler? Do parents lose by their son becoming a better, wiser man? Does a wife lose by the spiritual growth of her husband?

Miss Mahr. You are both right and wrong. . . . Your parents have a different standard from you. Kitty's again, differs from theirs. It seems to me that in this we cannot judge for them.

John. Yes, but you have always said yourself that one should not allow one's self to be ruled by the opinion of others—that one ought to be independent?

Miss Mahr. You have often said to me that you foresee a new, a nobler state of fellowship between man and woman.

John. Yes, I feel that it will come some time—a relationship in which the human will preponderate over the animal tie. Animal will no longer be united to animal, but one human being to another. Friendship is the foundation on which this love will rise, beautiful, unchangeable, a miraculous structure. And I foresee more than this—something nobler, richer, freer still.

Miss Mahr. But will you get anyone, except me, to believe this? Will this prevent Kitty's grieving herself to death? . . . Don't let us speak of ourselves at all. Let us suppose, quite generally, the feeling of a new, more perfect relationship between two people to exist, as it were prophetically. It is only a feeling, a young and all too tender plant which must be carefully watched and guarded. Don't you think so, Dr. Vockerat? That this plant should come to perfection during our lifetime is not to be expected. We shall not see or taste its fruits. But we may help to propagate it for future generations. I could imagine a person accepting this as a life-task.

John. And hence you conclude that we must part.

Miss Mahr. I did not mean to speak of ourselves. But it is as you say . . . we must part. Another idea . . . had sometimes suggested itself to me too . . . momentarily. But I could not entertain it now. I too have felt as if it were the presentiment of better things. And since then the old aim seems to me too poor a one for us—too common, to tell the truth. It is like coming down from the mountain-top with its wide, free view, and feeling the narrowness, the nearness of everything in the valley.

Those who feel the narrow, stifling atmosphere must either die or leave. *Anna Mahr* is not made for the valley. She must live on the heights. But *John Vockerat,* harassed and whipped on by those who love him most, is unmanned, broken and crushed. He clings to *Anna Mahr* as one condemned to death.

John. Help me, Miss Anna! There is no manliness, no pride left in me. I am quite changed. At this moment I am not even the man I was before you came to us. The one feeling left in me is disgust and weariness of life. Everything has lost its worth to me, is soiled, polluted, desecrated, dragged through the mire. When I think what you, your presence, your words made me, I feel that if I cannot be that again, then—then all the rest no longer means anything to me. I draw a line through it all and—*close my account.*

Miss Mahr. It grieves me terribly, Dr. Vockerat, to see you like this. I hardly know how I am to help you. But one thing you ought to remember—that we foresaw this. We knew that we must be prepared for this sooner or later. *John.* Our prophetic feeling of a new, a free existence, a far-off state of blessedness—that feeling we will keep. It shall never be forgotten, though it may never be realized. It shall be my guiding light; when this light is extinguished, my life will be extinguished too. *Miss Mahr.* John! one word more! This ring—was taken from the finger of a dead woman, who had followed her—her husband to Siberia—and faithfully shared his suffering to the end. Just the opposite to our case. . . . It is the only ring I have ever worn. Its story is a thing to think of when one feels weak. And when you look at it—in hours of weakness—then—think of her—who, far away—lonely like yourself—is fighting the same secret fight—Good-bye!

But John lacks the strength for the fight. Life to him is too lonely, too empty, too unbearably desolate. He has to die—a suicide.

What wonderful grasp of the deepest and most hidden tones of the human soul! What significance in the bitter truth that those who struggle for an ideal, those who attempt to cut themselves loose from the old, from the thousand fetters that hold them down, are doomed to lonely lives!

Gerhart Hauptmann has dedicated this play "to those who have lived this life." And there are many, oh, so many who must live this life, torn out root and all from the soil of their birth, of their surroundings and past. The ideal they see only in the distance—sometimes quite near, again in the far-off distance. These are the lonely lives.

This drama also emphasizes the important point that not only the parents and the wife of *John Vockerat* fail to understand him, but even his own comrade, one of his own world, the painter *Braun,*—the type of fanatical revolutionist who scorns human weaknesses and ridicules those who make concessions and compromises. But not even this arch-revolutionist can grasp the needs of *John.* Referring to his chum's friendship with *Anna, Braun* upbraids him. He charges *John* with causing his wife's unhappiness and hurting the feelings of his parents. This very man who, as a propagandist, demands that every one live up to his ideal, is quick to condemn his friend when the latter, for the first time in his life, tries to be consistent, to be true to his own innermost being.

The revolutionary, the social and human significance of "Lonely Lives" consists in the lesson that the real revolutionist,—the dreamer, the creative artist, the iconoclast in whatever line,—is fated to be misunderstood, not only by his own kin, but often by his own comrades. That is the doom of all great spirits: they are detached from their environment. Theirs is a lonely life—the life of the transition stage, the hardest and the most difficult period for the individual as well as for a people.

THE WEAVERS

When "The Weavers" first saw the light, pandemonium broke out in the "land of thinkers and poets." "What!" cried Philistia, "workingmen, dirty, emaciated and starved, to be placed on the stage! Poverty, in all its ugliness, to be presented as an after-dinner amusement? That is too much!"

Indeed it is too much for the self-satisfied bourgeoisie to be brought face to face with the horrors of the weaver's existence. It is too much, because of the truth and reality that thunders in the placid ears of society a terrific *J'accuse!*

Gerhart Hauptmann is a child of the people; his grandfather was a weaver, and the only way his father could escape the fate of his parents was by leaving his trade and opening an inn. Little Gerhart's vivid and impressionable mind must have received many pictures from the stories told about the life of the weavers. Who knows but that the social panorama which Hauptmann subsequently gave to the world, had not slumbered in the soul of the child, gaining form and substance as he grew to manhood. At any rate "The Weavers," like the canvases of Millet and the heroic figures of Meunier, represent the epic of the age-long misery of labor, a profoundly stirring picture.

The background of "The Weavers" is the weaving district in Silesia, during the period of home industry—a gruesome sight of human phantoms, dragging on their emaciated existence almost by superhuman effort. Life is a tenacious force that clings desperately even to the most meager chance in an endeavor to assert itself. But what is mirrored in "The Weavers" is so appalling, so dismally hopeless that it stamps the damning brand upon our civilization.

One man and his hirelings thrive on the sinew and bone, on the very blood, of an entire community. The manufacturer *Dreissiger* spends more for cigars in a day than an entire family earns in a week. Yet so brutalizing, so terrible is the effect of wealth that neither pale hunger nor black despair can move the master.

There is nothing in literature to equal the cruel reality of the scene in the office of *Dreissiger,* when the weavers bring the finished cloth. For hours they are kept waiting in the stuffy place, waiting the pleasure of the rich employer after they had walked miles on an empty stomach and little sleep. For as one of the men says, "What's to hinder a weaver waitin' for an hour, or for a day? What else is he there for?"

Indeed what else, except to be always waiting in humility, to be exploited and degraded, always at the mercy of the few pence thrown to them after an endless wait.

Necessity knows no law. Neither does it know pride. The weavers, driven by the whip of hunger, bend their backs, beg and cringe before their "superior."

Weaver's wife. No one can't call me idle, but I am not fit now for what I once was. I've twice had a miscarriage. As to John, he's but a poor creature. He's been to the shepherd at Zerlau, but he couldn't do him no good, and . . . you can't do more than you've strength for. . . . We works as hard as ever we can. This many a week I've been at it till far into the night. An' we'll keep our heads above water right enough if I can just get a bit o' strength into me. But you must have pity on us, Mr. Pfeifer, sir. You'll please be so very kind as to let me have a few pence on the next job, sir? Only a few pence, to buy bread with. We can't get no more credit. We've a lot o' little ones.

"Suffer little children to come unto me." Christ loves the children of the poor. The more the better. Why, then, care if they starve? Why care if they faint away with hunger, like the little boy in *Dreissiger's* office? For "little Philip is one of nine and the tenth's coming, and the rain comes through their roof—and the mother hasn't two shirts among the nine."

Who is to blame? Ask the Dreissigers. They will tell you, "The poor have too many children." Besides—

Dreissiger. It was nothing serious. The boy is all right again. But all the same it's a disgrace. The child's so weak that a puff of wind would blow him over. How people, how any parents can be so thoughtless is what passes my comprehension. Loading him with two heavy pieces of fustian to carry six good miles! No one would believe it that hadn't seen it. It simply means that I shall have to make a rule that no goods brought by children will be taken over. I sincerely trust that such things will not occur again.—Who gets all the blame for it? Why, of course the manufacturer. It's entirely our fault. If some poor little fellow sticks in the snow in winter and goes to sleep, a special correspondent arrives post-haste, and in two days we have a bloodcurdling story served up in all the papers. Is any blame laid on the father, the parents, that send such a child?—Not a bit of it. How should they be to blame? It's all the manufacturer's fault—he's made the scapegoat. They flatter the weaver, and give the manufacturer nothing but abuse—he's a cruel man, with a heart like a stone, a dangerous fellow, at whose calves every cur of a journalist may take a bite. He lives on the fat of the land, and pays the poor weavers starvation wages. In the flow of his eloquence the writer forgets to mention that such a man has his cares too and his sleepless nights; that he runs risks of which the workman never dreams; that he is often driven distracted by all the calculations he has to make, and all the different things he has to take into account; that he has to struggle for his very life against competition; and that no day passes without some annoyance or some loss. And think of the manufacturer's responsibilities, think of the numbers that depend on him, that look to him for their daily bread. No, No! none of you need wish yourselves in my shoes—you would soon have enough of it. You all saw how that fellow, that scoundrel Becker, behaved. Now he'll go and spread about all sorts of tales of my hardheartedness, of how my weavers are turned off for a mere trifle, without a moment's notice. Is that true? Am I so very unmerciful?

The weavers are too starved, too subdued, too terror-stricken not to accept *Dreissiger's* plea in his own behalf. What would become of these living corpses were it not for the rebels like *Becker,* to put fire, spirit, and hope in them? Verily the Beckers are dangerous.

Appalling as the scene in the office of *Dreissiger* is, the life in the home of the old weaver *Baumert* is even more terrible. His decrepit old wife, his idiotic son *August,* who still has to wind spools, his two daughters weaving their youth and bloom into the cloth, and *Ansorge,* the broken remnant of a heroic type of man, bent over his baskets, all live in cramped quarters lit up only by two small windows. They are waiting anxiously for the few pence old *Baumert* is to bring, that they may indulge in a long-missed meal. "What . . . what . . . what is to become of us if he don't come home?" laments *Mother Baumert.* "There is not so much as a handful o' salt in the house—not a bite o' bread, nor a bit o' wood for the fire."

But old *Baumert* has not forgotten his family. He brings them a repast, the first "good meal" they have had in two years. It is the meat of their faithful little dog, whom *Baumert* could not kill himself because he loved him so. But hunger knows no choice; *Baumert* had his beloved dog killed, because "a nice little bit o' meat like that does you a lot o' good."

It did not do old *Baumert* much good. His stomach, tortured and abused so long, rebelled, and the old man had to "give up the precious dog." And all this wretchedness, all this horror almost within sight of the palatial home of *Dreissiger,* whose dogs are better fed than his human slaves.

Man's endurance is almost limitless. Almost, yet not quite. For there comes a time when the *Baumerts,* even like their stomachs, rise in rebellion, when they hurl themselves, even though in blind fury, against the pillars of their prison house. Such a moment comes to the weavers, the most patient, docile and subdued of humanity, when stirred to action by the powerful poem read to them by the *Jaeger.*

The justice to us weavers dealt
Is bloody, cruel, and hateful;
Our life's one torture, long drawn out:
For Lynch law we'd be grateful.

Stretched on the rack day after day,
Heart sick and bodies aching,
Our heavy sighs their witness bear
To spirit slowly breaking.

The Dreissigers true hangmen are,
Servants no whit behind them;
Masters and men with one accord
Set on the poor to grind them.

You villains all, you brood of hell . . .
You fiends in fashion human,
A curse will fall on all like you,
Who prey on man and woman.

The suppliant knows he asks in vain,
Vain every word that's spoken,
"If not content, then go and starve—
Our rules cannot be broken."

Then think of all our woe and want,
O ye, who hear this ditty!
Our struggle vain for daily bread
Hard hearts would move to pity.

But pity's what you've never known—
You'd take both skin and clothing,
You cannibals, whose cruel deeds
Fill all good men with loathing.

The *Dreissigers,* however, will take no heed. Arrogant and secure in the possession of their stolen wealth, supported by the mouthpieces of the Church and the State, they feel safe from the wrath of the people—till it is too late. But when the storm breaks, they show the yellow streak and cravenly run to cover.

The weavers, roused at last by the poet's description of their condition, urged on by the inspiring enthusiasm of the *Beckers* and the *Jaegers,* become indifferent to the threats of the law and ignore the soft tongue of the dispenser of the pure word of God,—"the God who provides shelter and food for the birds and clothes the lilies of the field." Too long they had believed in Him. No wonder *Pastor Kittelhaus* is now at a loss to understand the weavers, heretofore "so patient, so humble, so easily led." The *Pastor* has to pay the price for his stupidity: the weavers have outgrown even him.

The spirit of revolt sweeps their souls. It gives them courage and strength to attack the rotten structure, to drive the thieves out of the temple, aye, even to rout the soldiers who come to save the sacred institution of capitalism. The women, too, are imbued with the spirit of revolt and become an avenging force. Not even the devout faith of *Old Hilse,* who attempts to stem the tide with his blind belief in his Saviour, can stay them.

Old Hilse. O Lord, we know not how to be thankful enough to Thee, for that Thou hast spared us this night again in Thy goodness . . . an' hast had pity on us . . . an' hast suffered us to take no harm. Thou art the All-merciful, an' we are poor, sinful children of men—that bad that we are not worthy to be trampled under Thy feet. Yet Thou art our loving Father, an' Thou wilt look upon us an' accept us for the sake of Thy dear Son, our Lord and Saviour Jesus Christ. "Jesus' blood and righteousness, Our covering is and glorious dress." An' if we're sometimes too sore cast down under Thy chastening—when the fire of Thy purification burns too ragin' hot—oh, lay it not to our charge; forgive us our sin. Give us patience, heavenly Father, that after all these sufferin's we may be made partakers of Thy eternal blessedness. Amen.

The tide is rushing on. *Luise, Old Hilse's* own daughter-in-law, is part of the tide.

Luise. You an' your piety an' religion—did they serve to keep the life in my poor children? In rags an' dirt they lay, all the four—it didn't as much as keep 'em dry. Yes! I sets up to be a mother, that's what I do—an' if you'd like to know it, that's why I'd send all the manufacturers to hell—because I am a mother!—Not one of the four could I keep in life! It was cryin' more than breathin' with me from the time each poor little thing came into the world till death took pity on it. The devil a bit you cared! You sat there prayin' and singin', and let me run about till my feet bled, tryin' to get one little drop o' skim milk. How many hundred nights has I lain an' racked my head to think what I could do to cheat the churchyard of my little one? What harm has a baby like that done that it must come to such a miserable end—eh? An' over there at Dittrich's they're bathed in wine an' washed in milk. No! you may talk as you like, but if they begins here, ten horses won't hold me back. An' what's more—if there's a rush on Dittrich's, you will see me in the forefront of it—an' pity the man as tries to prevent me—I've stood it long enough, so now you know it.

Thus the tide sweeps over *Old Hilse,* as it must sweep over every obstacle, every hindrance, once labor awakens to the consciousness of its solidaric power.

An epic of misery and revolt never before painted with such terrific force, such inclusive artistry. Hence its wide human appeal, its incontrovertible indictment and its ultra-revolutionary significance, not merely to Silesia or Germany, but to our whole pseudo-civilization built on the misery and exploitation of the wealth producers, of Labor. None greater, none more universal than this stirring, all-embracing message of the most humanly creative genius of our time—Gerhart Hauptmann.

THE SUNKEN BELL

The great versatility of Gerhart Hauptmann is perhaps nowhere so apparent as in "The Sunken Bell," the poetic fairy tale of the tragedy of Man, a tragedy as rich in symbolism as it is realistically true—a tragedy as old as mankind, as elemental as man's ceaseless struggle to cut loose from the rock of ages.

Heinrich, the master bell founder, is an idealist consumed by the fire of a great purpose. He has already set a hundred bells ringing in a hundred different towns, all singing his praises. But his restless spirit is not appeased. Ever it soars to loftier heights, always yearning to reach the sun.

Now once more he has tried his powers, and the new bell, the great Master Bell, is raised aloft,—only to sink into the mere, carrying its maker with it.

His old ideals are broken, and *Heinrich* is lost in the wilderness of life.

Weak and faint with long groping in the dark woods, and bleeding, *Heinrich* reaches the mountain top and there beholds *Rautendelein,* the spirit of freedom, that has allured him on in the work which he strove—"in one grand Bell, to weld the silver music of thy voice with the warm gold of a Sun-holiday. It should have been a master work! I failed, then wept I tears of blood." *Heinrich* returns to his faithful wife *Magda,* his children, and his village friends—to die. The bell that sank into the mere was not made for the heights—it was not fit to wake the answering echoes of the peaks!

Heinrich.

•   •   •   •   •   •   •   •   •   •   •

'Twas for the valley—not the mountain-top!
I choose to die. The service of the valleys
Charms me no longer, . . . since on the peak I stood.
Youth—a new youth—I'd need, if I should live:
Out of some rare and magic mountain flower
Marvelous juices I should need to press—
Heart-health, and strength, and the mad lust of triumph,
Steeling my hand to work none yet have dreamed of!

Rautendelein, the symbol of youth and freedom, the vision of new strength and expression, wakes *Heinrich* from his troubled sleep, kisses him back to life, and inspires him with faith and courage to work toward greater heights.

Heinrich leaves his wife, his hearth, his native place, and rises to the summit of his ideal, there to create, to fashion a marvel bell whose iron throat shall send forth

> The first waking peal
> Shall shake the skies—when, from the somber clouds
> That weighed upon us through the winter night,
> Rivers of jewels shall go rushing down
> Into a million hands outstretched to clutch!
> Then all who drooped, with sudden power inflamed,
> Shall bear their treasure homeward to their huts,
> There to unfurl, at last, the silken banners,
> Waiting—so long, so long—to be upraised.

. . . .

> And now the wondrous chime again rings out,
> Filling the air with such sweet, passionate sound
> As makes each breast to sob with rapturous pain.
> It sings a song, long lost and long forgotten,
> A song of home—a childlike song of Love,
> Born in the waters of some fairy well—
> Known to all mortals, and yet heard of none!

. . . .

> And as it rises, softly first, and low,
> The nightingale and dove seem singing, too;
> And all the ice in every human breast
> Is melted, and the hate, and pain, and woe,
> Stream out in tears.

Indeed a wondrous bell, as only those can forge who have reached the mountain top,—they who can soar upon the wings of their imagination high above the valley of the commonplace, above the dismal gray of petty consideration, beyond the reach of the cold, stifling grip of reality,—higher, ever higher, to kiss the sun-lit sky.

Heinrich spreads his wings. Inspired by the divine fire of *Rautendelein,* he all but reaches the pinnacle. But there is the *Vicar,* ready to wrestle with

the devil for a poor human soul; to buy it free, if need be, to drag it back to its
cage that it may never rise again in rebellion to the will of God.

The Vicar.

You shun the church, take refuge in the mountains;
This many a month you have not seen the home
Where your poor wife sits sighing, while, each day,
Your children drink their lonely mother's tears!

· · · · · · · · · · · ·

For this there is no name but madness,
And wicked madness. Yes. I speak the truth.
Here stand I, Master, overcome with horror
At the relentless cruelty of your heart.
Now Satan, aping God, hath dealt a blow—
Yes, I must speak my mind—a blow so dread
That even he must marvel at his triumph.
                    . . . Now—I have done.
Too deep, yea to the neck, you are sunk in sin!
Your Hell, decked out in beauty as high Heaven,
Shall hold you fast. I will not waste more words.
Yet mark this, Master: witches make good fuel,
Even as heretics, for funeral-pyres.
                    . . . Your ill deeds,
Heathen, and secret once, are now laid bare.
Horror they wake, and soon there shall come hate.

· · · · · · · · · · · ·

Then, go your way! Farewell! My task is done.
The hemlock of your sin no man may hope
To rid your soul of. May God pity you!
But this remember! There's a word named rue!
And some day, some day, as your dreams you dream,
A sudden arrow, shot from out the blue,
Shall pierce your breast! And yet you shall not die,
Nor shall you live. In that dread day you'll curse
All you now cherish—God, the world, your work,
Your wretched self you'll curse. Then . . . think of me!
That bell shall ring again! Then think of me!

Barely does *Heinrich* escape the deadly clutch of outlived creeds, superstitions, and conventions embodied in the *Vicar*, than he is in the throes of other foes who conspire his doom.

Nature herself has decreed the death of *Heinrich*. For has not man turned his back upon her, has he not cast her off, scorned her beneficial offerings, robbed her of her beauty, devastated her charms and betrayed her trust—all for the ephemeral glow of artifice and sham? Hence Nature, too, is *Heinrich's* foe. Thus the Spirit of the Earth, with all its passions and lusts, symbolized in the Wood Sprite, and gross materialism in the person of the *Nickelmann*, drive the intruder back.

The Wood Sprite.

He crowds us from our hills. He hacks and hews,
Digs up our metals, sweats, and smelts, and brews.
The earth-man and the water-sprite he takes
To drag his burdens, and, to harness, breaks.

.   .   .   .

She steals my cherished flowers, my red-brown ores,
My gold, my precious stones, my resinous stores.
She serves him like a slave, by night and day.
'Tis he she kisses—us she keeps at bay.
Naught stands against him. Ancient trees he fells.
The earth quakes at his tread, and all the dells
Ring with the echo of his thunderous blows.
His crimson smithy furnace glows and shines
Into the depths of my most secret mines.
What he is up to, only Satan knows!

The Nickelmann.

Brekekekex! Hadst thou the creature slain,
A-rotting in the mere long since he had lain—
The maker of the bell, beside the bell.
And so when next I had wished to throw the stones,
The bell had been my box—the dice, his bones!

But even they are powerless to stem the tide of the Ideal: they are helpless in the face of *Heinrich's* new-born faith, of his burning passion to complete his task, and give voice to the thousand-throated golden peal.

Heinrich works and toils, and when doubt casts its black shadow athwart his path, *Rautendelein* charms back hope.   She alone has boundless faith in her Balder,—god of the joy of Life—for he is part of her, of the great glowing force her spirit breathed into the Heinrichs since Time was born—Liberty, redeemer of man.

Heinrich.

I am thy Balder?

Make me believe it—make me know it, child!

Give my faint soul the rapturous joy it needs,

To nerve it to its task.   For, as the hand,

Toiling with tong and hammer, on and on,

To hew the marble and to guide the chisel,

Now bungles here, now there, yet may not halt.

          . . . But—enough of this,

Still straight and steady doth the smoke ascend

From my poor human sacrifice to heaven.

Should now a Hand on high reject my gift,

Why, it may do so.   Then the priestly robe

Falls from my shoulder—by no act of mine;

While I, who erst upon the heights was set,

Must look my last on Horeb, and be dumb!

But now bring torches!   Lights!   And show thine Art!

Enchantress!   Fill the wine-cup!   We will drink!

Ay, like the common herd of mortal men,

With resolute hands our fleeting joy we'll grip!

Our unsought leisure we will fill with life,

Not waste it, as the herd, in indolence.

We will have music!

While *Heinrich* and *Rautendelein* are in the ecstasy of their love and work, the spirits weave their treacherous web—they threaten, they plead, they cling,—spirits whose pain and grief are harder to bear than the enmity or menace of a thousand foes.   Spirits that entwine one's heartstrings with tender touch, yet are heavier fetters, more oppressive than leaden weights. *Heinrich's* children, symbolizing regret that paralyzes one's creative powers, bring their mother's tears and with them a thousand hands to pull *Heinrich* down from his heights, back to the valley.

"The bell! The bell!" The old, long buried bell again ringing and tolling. Is it not the echo from the past? The superstitions instilled from birth, the prejudices that cling to man with cruel persistence, the conventions which fetter the wings of the idealist: the Old wrestling with the New for the control of man.

"The Sunken Bell" is a fairy tale in its poetic beauty and glow of radiant color. But stripped of the legendary and symbolic, it is the life story of every seeker for truth, of the restless spirit of rebellion ever striving onward, ever reaching out toward the sun-tipped mountain, ever yearning for a new-born light.

Too long had *Heinrich* lived in the valley. It has sapped his strength, has clipped his wings. "Too late! Thy heavy burdens weigh thee down; thy dead ⌐nes are too mighty for thee." *Heinrich* has to die. "He who has flown so high into the very Light, as thou hast flown, must perish, if he once fall back to earth."

Thus speak the worldly wise. As if death could still the burning thirst for light; as if the hunger for the ideal could ever be appeased by the thought of destruction! The worldly wise never feel the irresistible urge to dare the cruel fates. With the adder in Maxim Gorky's "Song of the Falcon" they sneer, "What is the sky? An empty place. . . . Why disturb the soul with the desire to soar into the sky? . . . Queer birds," they laugh at the falcons. "Not knowing the earth and grieving on it, they yearn for the sky, seeking for light in the sultry desert. For it is only a desert, with no food and no supporting place for a living body."

The Heinrichs are the social falcons, and though they perish when they fall to earth, they die in the triumphant glory of having beheld the sun, of having braved the storm, defied the clouds and mastered the air.

The sea sparkles in the glowing light, the waves dash against the shore. In their lion-like roar a song resounds about the proud falcons: "O daring Falcon, in the battle with sinister forces you lose your life. But the time will come when your precious blood will illumine, like the burning torch of truth, the dark horizon of man; when your blood shall inflame many brave hearts with a burning desire for freedom."

The time when the peals of Heinrich's Bell will call the strong and daring to battle for light and joy. "Hark! . . . 'Tis the music of the Sunbells' song! The Sun . . . the Sun . . . draws near!" . . . and though "the night is long," dawn breaks, its first rays falling on the dying Heinrichs.

FRANK WEDEKIND

SPRING'S AWAKENING

FRANK WEDEKIND is perhaps the most daring dramatic spirit in Germany. Coming to the fore much later than Sudermann and Hauptmann, he did not follow in their path, but set out in quest of new truths. More boldly than any other dramatist Frank Wedekind has laid bare the shams of morality in reference to sex, especially attacking the ignorance surrounding the sex life of the child and its resultant tragedies.

Wedekind became widely known through his great drama "Spring's Awakening," which he called a tragedy of childhood, dedicating the work to parents and teachers. Verily an appropriate dedication, because parents and teachers are, in relation to the child's needs, the most ignorant and mentally indolent class. Needless to say, this element entirely failed to grasp the social significance of Wedekind's work. On the contrary, they saw in it an invasion of their traditional authority and an outrage on the sacred rights of parenthood.

The critics also could see naught in Wedekind, except a base, perverted, almost diabolic nature bereft of all finer feeling. But professional critics seldom see below the surface; else they would discover beneath the grin and satire of Frank Wedekind a sensitive soul, deeply stirred by the heart-rending tragedies about him. Stirred and grieved especially by the misery and torture of the child,—the helpless victim unable to explain the forces germinating in its nature, often crushed and destroyed by mock modesty, sham decencies, and the complacent morality that greet its blind gropings.

Never was a more powerful indictment hurled against society, which out of sheer hypocrisy and cowardice persists that boys and girls must grow up in ignorance of their sex functions, that they must be sacrificed on the altar of stupidity and convention which taboo the enlightenment of the child in questions of such elemental importance to health and well-being.

The most criminal phase of the indictment, however, is that it is generally the most promising children who are sacrificed to sex ignorance and to the total lack of appreciation on the part of teachers of the latent qualities and tendencies in the child: the one slaying the body and soul, the other paralyzing the function of the brain; and both conspiring to give the world mental and physical mediocrities.

"Spring's Awakening" is laid in three acts and fourteen scenes, consisting almost entirely of dialogues among the children. So close is Wedekind to the soul of the child that he succeeds in unveiling before our eyes, with a most gripping touch, its joys and sorrows, its hopes and despair, its struggles and tragedies.

The play deals with a group of school children just entering the age of puberty,—imaginative beings speculating about the mysteries of life. *Wendla,* sent to her grave by her loving but prudish mother, is an exquisite, lovable child; *Melchior,* the innocent father of *Wendla's* unborn baby, is a gifted boy whose thirst for knowledge leads him to inquire into the riddle of life, and to share his observations with his school chums,—a youth who, in a free and intelligent atmosphere, might have developed into an original thinker. That such a boy should be punished as a moral pervert, only goes to prove the utter unfitness of our educators and parents. *Moritz, Melchior's* playfellow, is driven to suicide because he cannot pass his examinations, thanks to our stupid and criminal system of education which consists in cramming the mind to the bursting point.

Wedekind has been accused of exaggerating his types, but any one familiar with child life knows that every word in "Spring's Awakening" is vividly true. The conversation between *Melchior* and *Moritz,* for instance, is typical of all boys not mentally inert.

Melchior. I'd like to know why we really are on earth!

Moritz. I'd rather be a cab-horse than go to school!—Why do we go to school?—We go to school so that somebody can examine us!—And why do they examine us?—In order that we may fail. Seven must fail, because the upper classroom will hold only sixty.—I feel so queer since Christmas.— The devil take me, if it were not for Papa, I'd pack my bundle and go to Altoona, to-day!

Moritz. Do you believe, Melchior, that the feeling of shame in man is only a product of his education?

Melchior. I was thinking over that for the first time the day before yesterday. It seems to me deeply rooted in human nature. Only think, you must appear entirely clothed before your best friend. You wouldn't do so if he didn't do the same thing.—Therefore, it's more or less of a fashion.

Moritz. Have you experienced it yet?

Melchior. What?

Moritz. How do you say it?

Melchior. Manhood's emotion?

Moritz. M—'hm.

Melchior. Certainly.

Moritz. I also . . .

Melchior. I've known that for a long while!—Almost for a year.

Moritz. I was startled as if by lightning.

Melchior. Did you dream?

Moritz. Only for a little while—of legs in light blue tights, that strode over the cathedral—to be correct, I thought they wanted to go over it. I only saw them for an instant.

Melchior. George Zirschnitz dreamed of his mother.

Moritz. Did he tell you that? . . . I thought I was incurable. I believed I was suffering from an inward hurt.—Finally I became calm enough to begin to jot down the recollections of my life. Yes, yes, dear Melchior, the last three weeks have been a Gethsemane for me. . . . Truly they play a remarkable game with us. And we're expected to give thanks for it. I don't remember to have had any longing for this kind of excitement. Why didn't they let me sleep peacefully until all was still again. My dear parents might have had a hundred better children. I came here, I don't know how, and must be responsible myself for not staying away.—Haven't you often wondered, Melchior, by what means we were brought into this whirl?

Melchior. Don't you know that yet either, Moritz?

Moritz. How should I know it? I see how the hens lay eggs, and hear that Mamma had to carry me under her heart. But is that enough? . . . I have gone through Meyer's "Little Encyclopedia" from A to Z. Words—nothing but words and words! Not a single plain explanation. Oh, this feeling of shame!— What good to me is an encyclopedia that won't answer me concerning the most important question in life?

Yes, of what good is an encyclopedia or the other wise books to the quivering, restless spirit of the child? No answer anywhere, least of all from your own mother, as *Wendla* and many another like her have found out.

The girl, learning that her sister has a new baby, rushes to her mother to find out how it came into the world.

Wendla. I have a sister who has been married for two and a half years, I myself have been made an aunt for the third time, and I haven't the least idea how it all comes about—Don't be cross, Mother dear, don't be cross! Whom in the world should I ask but you! Please tell me, dear Mother! Tell me, dear Mother! I am ashamed for myself. Please, Mother, speak! Don't scold me for asking you about it. Give me an answer—How does it happen?—How does it all come about?—You cannot really deceive yourself that I, who am fourteen years old, still believe in the stork.

Frau Bergmann. Good Lord, child, but you are peculiar!—What ideas you have!—I really can't do that!

Wendla. But why not, Mother?—Why not?—It can't be anything ugly if everybody is delighted over it!

Frau Bergmann. O—O God, protect me!—I deserve—Go get dressed, child, go get dressed.

Wendla. I'll go—And suppose your child went out and asked the chimney sweep?

Frau Bergmann. But that would be madness!—Come here, child, come here, I'll tell you! I'll tell you everything—. . . In order to have a child— one must love—the man—to whom one is married—love him, I tell you—as one can only love a man! One must love him so much with one's whole heart, so—so that one can't describe it! One must love him, Wendla, as you at your age are still unable to love—Now you know it!

How much *Wendla* knew, her mother found out when too late.

Wendla and *Melchior,* overtaken by a storm, seek shelter in a haystack, and are drawn by what *Melchior* calls the "first emotion of manhood" and curiosity into each other's arms. Six months later *Wendla's* mother discovers that her child is to become a mother. To save the family honor, the girl is promptly placed in the hands of a quack who treats her for chlorosis.

Wendla. No, Mother, no! I know it. I feel it. I haven't chlorosis. I have dropsy—I won't get better. I have the dropsy, I must die, Mother—O, Mother, I must die!

Frau Bergmann. You must not die, child! You must not die—Great heavens, you must not die!

Wendla. But why do you weep so frightfully, then?

Frau Bergmann. You must not die, child! You haven't the dropsy, you have a child, girl! You have a child! Oh, why did you do that to me?

Wendla. I haven't done anything to you.

Frau Bergmann. Oh, don't deny it any more, Wendla!—I know everything. See, I didn't want to say a word to you.—Wendla, my Wendla—!

Wendla. But it's not possible, Mother. . . . I have loved nobody in the world as I do you, Mother.

The pathos of it, that such a loving mother should be responsible for the death of her own child! Yet *Frau Bergmann* is but one of the many good, pious mothers who lay their children to "rest in God," with the inscription on the tombstone: "Wendla Bergmann, born May 5th, 1878, died from chlorosis, Oct. 27, 1892. Blessed are the pure of heart."

Melchior, like *Wendla,* was also "pure of heart"; yet how was he "blessed"? Surely not by his teachers who, discovering his essay on the mystery of life, expel the boy from school. Only Wedekind could inject such grim humor into the farce of education—the smug importance of the faculty of the High School sitting under the portraits of Rousseau and Pestalozzi, and pronouncing judgment on their "immoral" pupil *Melchior.*

Rector Sonnenstich. Gentlemen: We cannot help moving the expulsion of our guilty pupil before the National Board of Education; there are the strongest reasons why we cannot: we cannot, because we must expiate the misfortune which has fallen upon us already; we cannot, because of our need to protect ourselves from similar blows in the future; we cannot, because we must chastise our guilty pupil for the demoralizing influence he exerted upon his classmates; we cannot, above all, because we must hinder him from exerting the same influence upon his remaining classmates. We cannot ignore the charge—and this, gentlemen, is possibly the weightiest of all—on any pretext concerning a ruined career, because it is our duty to protect ourselves from an epidemic of suicide similar to that which has broken out recently in various grammar schools, and which until to-day has mocked all attempts of the teachers to shackle it by any means known to advanced education. . . . We see ourselves under the necessity of judging the guilt-laden that we may not be judged guilty ourselves. . . . Are you the author of this obscene manuscript?

Melchior. Yes—I request you, sir, to show me anything obscene in it.

Sonnenstich. You have as little respect for the dignity of your assembled teachers as you have a proper appreciation of mankind's innate sense of shame which belongs to a moral world.

Melchior's mother, a modern type, has greater faith in her child than in school education. But even she cannot hold out against the pressure of public opinion; still less against the father of *Melchior,* a firm believer in authority and discipline.

Herr Gabor. Anyone who can write what Melchior wrote must be rotten to the core of his being. The mark is plain. A half-healthy nature wouldn't do such a thing. None of us are saints. Each of us wanders from the straight path. His writing, on the contrary, tramples on principles. His writing is no evidence of a chance slip in the usual way; it sets forth with dreadful plainness and a frankly definite purpose that natural longing, that propensity for immorality, because it is immorality. His writing manifests that exceptional state of spiritual corruption which we jurists classify under the term "moral imbecility."

Between the parents and the educators, *Melchior* is martyred even as *Wendla.* He is sent to the House of Correction; but being of sturdier stock than the girl, he survives.

Not so his chum *Moritz.* Harassed by the impelling forces of his awakened nature, and unable to grapple with the torturous tasks demanded by his "educators" at the most critical period of his life, *Moritz* fails in the examinations. He cannot face his parents: they have placed all their hope in him, and have lashed him, by the subtle cruelty of gratitude, to the grindstone till his brain reeled. *Moritz* is the third victim in the tragedy, the most convenient explanation of which is given by *Pastor Kahlbauch* in the funeral sermon.

Pastor Kahlbauch. He who rejects the grace with which the Everlasting Father has blessed those born in sin, he shall die a spiritual death!—He, however, who in willful carnal abnegation of God's proper honor, lives for and serves evil, shall die the death of the body!—Who, however, wickedly throws away from him the cross which the All Merciful has laid upon him for his sins, verily, verily, I say unto you, he shall die the everlasting death! Let us, however, praise the All Gracious Lord and thank Him for His inscrutable grace in order that we may travel the thorny path more and more surely. For as truly as this one died a triple death, as truly will the Lord God conduct the righteous unto happiness and everlasting life. . . .

It is hardly necessary to point out the revolutionary significance of this extraordinary play. It speaks powerfully for itself. One need only add that "Spring's Awakening" has done much to dispel the mist enveloping the paramount issue of sex in the education of the child. To-day it is conceded even by conservative elements that the conspiracy of silence has been a fatal mistake. And while sponsors of the Church and of moral fixity still clamor for the good old methods, the message of Wedekind is making itself felt throughout the world, breaking down the barriers.

The child is the unit of the race, and only through its unhampered unfoldment can humanity come into its heritage. "Spring's Awakening" is one of the great forces of modern times that is paving the way for the birth of a free race.

THE FRENCH DRAMA

MAETERLINCK

To those who are conversant with the works of Maeterlinck it may seem rather far-fetched to discuss him from the point of view of revolutionary and social significance. Above all, Maeterlinck is the portrayer of the remote, the poet of symbols; therefore it may seem out of place to bring him down to earth, to simplify him, or to interpret his revolutionary spirit. To some extent these objections have considerable weight; but on the other hand, if one keeps in mind that only those who go to the remote are capable of understanding the obvious, one will readily see how very significant Maeterlinck is as a revolutionizing factor. Besides, we have Maeterlinck's own conception of the significance of the revolutionary spirit. In a very masterly article called "The Social Revolution," he discusses the objection on the part of the conservative section of society to the introduction of revolutionary methods. He says that they would like us to "go slow"; that they object to the use of violence and the forcible overthrow of the evils of society. And Maeterlinck answers in these significant words:

"We are too ready to forget that the headsmen of misery are less noisy, less theatrical, but infinitely more numerous, more cruel and active than those of the most terrible revolutions."

Maeterlinck realizes that there are certain grievances in society, iniquitous conditions which demand immediate solution, and that if we do not solve them with the readiest and quickest methods at our command, they will react upon society and upon life a great deal more terribly than even the most terrible revolutions. No wonder, then, that his works were put under the ban by the Catholic Church which forever sees danger in light and emancipation. Surely if Maeterlinck were not primarily the spokesman of truth, he would be embraced by the Catholic Church.

In "Monna Vanna" Maeterlinck gives a wonderful picture of the new woman—not the new woman as portrayed in the newspapers, but the new woman as a reborn, regenerated spirit; the woman who has emancipated herself from her narrow outlook upon life, and detached herself from the confines of the home; the woman, in short, who has become race-conscious and therefore understands that she is a unit in the great ocean of life, and that she must take her place as an independent factor in order to rebuild and remold life. In proportion as she learns to become race-conscious, does she become a factor in the reconstruction of society, valuable to herself, to her children, and to the race.

Pisa is subdued by the forces of Florence; it is beaten and conquered. The city is in danger of being destroyed, and the people exposed to famine and annihilation. There is only one way of saving Pisa. *Marco Colonna,* the father of the Commander of Pisa, brings the ultimatum of the enemy:

Marco. Know, then, that I saw Prinzivalle and spoke with him. . . . I thought to find some barbarian, arrogant and heavy, always covered with blood or plunged in drunken stupor; at best, the madman they have told us of, whose spirit was lit up at times, upon the battlefield, by dazzling flashes of brilliance, coming no man knows whence. I thought to meet the demon of combat, blind, unreasoning, vain and cruel, faithless and dissolute. . . . I found a man who bowed before me as a loving disciple bows before the master. He is lettered, eager for knowledge, and obedient to the voice of wisdom. . . . He loves not war; his smile speaks of understanding and gentle humanity. He seeks the reason of passions and events. He looks into his own heart; he is endowed with conscience and sincerity, and it is against his will that he serves a faithless State. . . . I have told you that Prinzivalle seems wise, that he is humane and reasonable. But where is the wise man that hath not his private madness, the good man to whom no monstrous idea has ever come? On one side is reason and pity and justice; on the other—ah! *there* is desire and passion and what you will—the insanity into which we all fall at times. I have fallen into it myself, and shall, belike, again—so have you. Man is made in that fashion. A grief which should not be within the experience of man is on the point of touching you. . . . Hearken: this great convoy, the victuals that I have seen, wagons running over with corn, others full of wine and fruit; flocks of sheep and herds of cattle, enough to feed a city for months; all these tuns of powder and bars of lead, with which you may vanquish Florence and make Pisa lift her head—all this will enter the city to-night, . . . if you send in exchange, to give her up to Prinzivalle until to-morrow's dawn, . . . for he will send her back when the first faint gray shows in the sky, . . . only, he exacts that, in sign of victory and submission, she shall come alone, and her cloak for all her covering. . . .

Guido. Who? Who shall thus come?

Marco. Giovanna.

Guido. My wife? Vanna?

Marco. Ay, your Vanna.

Guido Colonna, in the consciousness that the woman belongs to him, that no man may even look, with desire, upon her dazzling beauty, resents this mortal insult. He is willing that all the other women should face danger, that the little children of Pisa should be exposed to hunger and destruction, rather than that he give up his possession. But *Monna Vanna* does not hesitate. When she is before the issue of saving her people, she does not stop to consider. She goes into the enemy's tent, as a child might go, without consciousness of self, imbued solely with the impulse to save her people.

The meeting of *Monna Vanna* and *Prinzivalle* is an exquisite interpretation of love—the sweetness, purity, and fragrance of *Prinzivalle's* love for the woman of his dream—the one he had known when she was but a child, and who remained an inspiring vision all through his career. He knows he cannot reach her; he also knows that he will be destroyed by the political intriguers of Florence, and he stakes his all on this one step to satisfy the dream of his life to see *Vanna* and in return to save Pisa.

Prinzivalle. Had there come ten thousand of you into my tent, all clad alike, all equally fair, ten thousand sisters whom even their mother would not know apart, I should have risen, should have taken your hand, and said, "This is she!" Is it not strange that a beloved image can live thus in a man's heart? For yours lived so in mine that each day it changed as in real life—the image of to-day replaced that of yesterday—it blossomed out, it became always fairer; and the years adorned it with all that they add to a child that grows in grace and beauty. But when I saw you again, it seemed to me at first that my eyes deceived me. My memories were so fair and so fond—but they had been too slow and too timid—they had not dared to give you all the splendor which appeared so suddenly to dazzle me. I was as a man that recalled to mind a flower he had but seen in passing through a garden on a gray day, and should be suddenly confronted with a hundred thousand as fair in a field bathed with sunshine. I saw once more your hair, your brow, your eyes, and I found all the soul of the face I had adored—but how its beauty shames that which I had treasured in silence through endless days, through years whose only light was a memory that had taken too long a road and found itself outshone by the reality! . . . Ah! I knew not too well what I meant to do. I felt that I was lost—and I desired to drag with me all I could. . . . And I hated you, because of the love. . . . Yes, I should have gone to the end had it not been *you*. . . . Yet any other would have seemed odious to me—you yourself would have had to be other than you are. . . . I lose my reason when I think of it. . . . One word would have been enough that was different from your words—one gesture that was not yours—the slightest thing would have inflamed my hate and let loose the monster. But when I saw you, I saw in that same moment that it was impossible.

Vanna. I felt a change, too. . . . I marveled that I could speak to you as I have spoken since the first moment. . . . I am silent by nature—I have never spoken thus to any man, unless it be to Marco, Guido's father. . . . And even with him it is not the same. He has a thousand dreams that take up all his mind, . . . and we have talked but a few times. The others have always a desire in their eyes that will not suffer one to tell them that one loves them and would fain know what they have in their hearts. In your eyes, too, a longing burns; but it is not the same—it does not affright me nor fill me with loathing. I felt at once that I knew you before I remembered that I had ever seen you. . . .

Vanna, awed by the character and personality of this despised and hated outlaw, pleads with him to come with her to Pisa under the protection of herself and her husband. She is sure that he will be safe with them, and that he will be hailed as the redeemer of the people of Pisa. Like innocent children they walk to their doom.

Vanna is honored by the people whom she has saved, but scorned by her husband who, like the true male, does not credit her story.

Vanna. Hear me, I say! I have never lied—but to-day, above all days, I tell the deepest truth, the truth that can be told but once and brings life or death. . . . Hearken, Guido, then—and look upon me, if you have never known me until this hour, the first and only hour when you have it in your power to love me as I would be loved. I speak in the name of our life, of all that I am, of all that you are to me. . . . Be strong enough to believe that which is incredible. This man has spared my honor. . . . He had all power—I was given over to him. Yet he has not touched me—I have issued from his tent as I might from my brother's house. . . . I gave him one only kiss upon the brow—and he gave it me again.

Guido. Ah, that was what you were to tell us—that was the miracle! Ay, already, at the first words, I divined something beneath them that I understood not. . . . It passed me like a flash—I took no heed of it. . . . But I see now that I must look more closely. So, when he had you in his tent, alone, with a cloak for all your covering, all night long, you say he spared you? . . . Am I a man to believe that the stars are fragments of hellebore, or that one may drop something into a well and put out the moon? ... What! a man desires you so utterly that he will betray his country, stake all that he has for one single night, ruin himself forever, and do it basely, do such a deed as no man ever thought to do before him, and make the world uninhabitable to himself forever! And this man has you there in his tent, alone and defenseless, and he has but this single night that he has bought at such a price—and he contents himself with a kiss upon the brow, and comes even hither to make us give him credence! No, let us reason fairly and not too long mock at misfortune. If he asked but that, what need was there that he should plunge a whole people into sadness, sink me in an abyss of misery such that I have come from it crushed and older by ten years? Ah! Had he craved but a kiss upon the brow, he might have saved us without torturing us so! He had but to come like a god to our rescue. ... But a kiss upon the brow is not demanded and prepared for after his fashion. ... The truth is found in our cries of anguish and despair. ...

It is only at this psychological moment, a moment that sometimes changes all our conceptions, all our thoughts, our very life, that *Monna Vanna* feels the new love for *Prinzivalle* stirring in her soul, a love that knows no doubt. The conception of such a love is revolutionary in the scope of its possibilities—a love that is pregnant with the spirit of daring, of freedom, that lifts woman out of the ordinary and inspires her with the strength and joy of molding a new and free race.

ROSTAND

CHANTECLER

In view of the progress the modern drama has made as an interpreter of social ideas and portrayer of the human struggle against internal and external barriers, it is difficult to say what the future may bring in the way of great dramatic achievement. So far, however, there is hardly anything to compare with "Chantecler" in philosophic depth and poetic beauty.

Chantecler is the intense idealist, whose mission is light and truth. His soul is aglow with deep human sympathies, and his great purpose in life is to dispel the night. He keeps aloof from mediocrity; indeed, he has little knowledge of his immediate surroundings. Like all great visionaries, *Chantecler* is human, "all too human"; therefore subject to agonizing soul depressions and doubts. Always, however, he regains confidence and strength when he is close to the soil; when he feels the precious sap of the earth surging through his being. At such times he feels the mysterious power that gives strength to proclaim the truth, to call forth the golden glory of the day.

The *pheasant hen* is the eternal female, bewitchingly beautiful, but self-centered and vain. True to her destiny, she must possess the man and is jealous of everything that stands between her and him she loves. She therefore employs every device to kill *Chantecler's* faith in himself, for, as she tells him, "You can be all in all to me, but nothing to the dawn."

The *blackbird* is the modernist who has become blasé, mentally and spiritually empty. He is a cynic and scoffer; without principle or sincerity himself, he sees only small and petty intentions in everybody else.

Patou, true and stanch, is the symbol of honest conviction and simplicity of soul. He loathes the blackbird because he sees in him the embodiment of a shallow, superficial modernity, a modernity barren of all poetic vision, which aims only at material success and tinseled display, without regard for worth, harmony or peace.

The *peacock* is the overbearing, conceited, intellectual charlatan; the spokesman of our present-day culture; the idle prater of "art for art's sake." As such he sets the style and pace for the idle pursuits of an idle class.

The *guinea hen* is none other than our most illustrious society lady. Sterile of mind and empty of soul, she flits from one social function to another, taking up every fad, clinging to the coattails of every newcomer, provided he represent station and prestige. She is the slave of fashion, the imitator of ideas, the silly hunter after effect—in short, the parasite upon the labor and efforts of others.

The *night birds* are the ignorant, stupid maintainers of the old. They detest the light because it exposes their mediocrity and stagnation. They hate *Chantecler* because, as the old owl remarks, "Simple torture it is to hear a brazen throat forever reminding you of what you know to be only too true!" This is a crime mediocrity never forgives, and it conspires to kill *Chantecler*.

The *woodpecker* is our very learned college professor. Dignified and important, he loudly proclaims the predigested food of his college as the sole source of all wisdom.

The *toads* represent the cringing, slimy hangers-on, the flunkies and lickspittles who toady for the sake of personal gain.

"Chantecler," then, is a scathing arraignment of the emptiness of our so-called wise and cultured, of the meanness of our conventional lies, the petty jealousies of the human breed in relation to each other. At the same time "Chantecler" characterizes the lack of understanding for, and appreciation of, the ideal and the idealists—the mob spirit, whether on top or at the bottom, using the most cruel and contemptible methods to drag the idealist down; to revile and persecute him—aye, even to kill him—for the unpardonable sin of proclaiming the ideal. They cannot forgive *Chantecler* for worshiping the sun:

Chantecler.
Blaze forth in glory! . . .
O thou that driest the tears of the meanest among weeds
And dost of a dead flower make a living butterfly—
Thy miracle, wherever almond-trees
Shower down the wind their scented shreds,
Dead petals dancing in a living swarm—
I worship thee, O Sun! whose ample light,
Blessing every forehead, ripening every fruit,
Entering every flower and every hovel,
Pours itself forth and yet is never less,
Still spending and unspent—like mother's love!

I sing of thee, and will be thy high priest,
Who disdainest not to glass thy shining face
In the humble basin of blue suds,
Or see the lightning of thy last farewell
Reflected in an humble cottage pane!

.   .   .   .

Glory to thee in the vineyards! Glory to thee in the
    fields!
Glory among the grass and on the roofs,
In eyes of lizards and on wings of swans,—
Artist who making splendid the great things
Forgets not to make exquisite the small!
'Tis thou that, cutting out a silhouette,
To all thou beamest on dost fasten this dark twin,
Doubling the number of delightful shapes,
Appointing to each thing its shadow,
More charming often than itself.

I praise thee, Sun! Thou sheddest roses on the air,
Diamonds on the stream, enchantment on the hill;
A poor dull tree thou takest and turnest to green rapture,
O Sun, without whose golden magic—things
Would be no more than what they are!

In the atmosphere of persecution and hatred *Chantecler* continues to hope and to work for his sublime mission of bringing the golden day. But his passion for the *pheasant hen* proves his Waterloo. It is through her that he grows weak, disclosing his secret. Because of her he attends the silly five o'clock function at the *guinea hen's,* and is involved in a prize fight. His passion teaches him to understand life and the frailties of his fellow creatures. He learns the greatest of all truths,—that "it is the struggle for, rather than the attainment of, the ideal, which must forever inspire the sincere, honest idealist." Indeed, it is life which teaches *Chantecler* that if he cannot wake the dawn, he must rouse mankind to greet the sun.

Chantecler finds himself in a trying situation when he comes into the gathering at the *guinea hen's* five o'clock tea, to meet the pompous, overbearing cocks representing the various governments. When he arrives in the midst of these distinguished society people, he is plied with the query, "How do you sing? Do you sing the Italian school or the French school or the German school?" Poor *Chantecler,* in the simplicity of his idealism, replies, "I don't know how I sing, but I know why I sing." Why need the chanteclers know how they sing? They represent the truth, which needs no stylish clothes or expensive feathers. That is the difference between truth and falsehood. Falsehood must deck herself out beyond all semblance of nature and reality.

Chantecler. I say ... that these resplendent gentlemen are manufactured wares, the work of merchants with highly complex brains, who to fashion a ridiculous chicken have taken a wing from that one, a topknot from this. I say that in such Cocks nothing remains of the true Cock. They are Cocks of shreds and patches, idle bric-a-brac, fit to figure in a catalogue, not in a barnyard with its decent dunghill and its dog. I say that those befrizzled, beruffled, bedeviled Cocks were never stroked and cherished by Nature's maternal hand. ... And I add that the whole duty of a Cock is to be an embodied crimson cry! And when a Cock is not that, it matters little that his comb be shaped like a toadstool, or his quills twisted like a screw, he will soon vanish and be heard of no more, having been nothing but a variety of a variety!

The *Game Cock* appears. He greets *Chantecler* with the announcement that he is the Champion fighter, that he has killed so and so many Cocks in one day and an equal number on other occasions. *Chantecler* replies simply, "I have never killed anything. But as I have at different times succored, defended, protected this one and that, I might perhaps be called, in my fashion, brave."

The fight begins. *Chantecler* is wounded and about to succumb, when suddenly all the guests present rush to *Chantecler* for protection: the common enemy, the *Hawk* is seen to approach. *Chantecler* mistakes the cowardice of those who come to seek his aid, for friendship; but the moment the danger is over, the crowd again circles around the fighters, inciting the *Game Cock* to kill *Chantecler*. But at the critical moment the *Game Cock* mortally wounds himself with his own spurs, and is jeered and driven off the scene by the same mob that formerly cheered him on. *Chantecler,* weak and exhausted from loss of blood, disillusioned and stung to the very soul, follows the *pheasant hen* to the Forest.

Soon he finds himself a henpecked husband: he may not crow to his heart's content any more, he may not wake the sun, for his lady love is jealous. The only time he can crow is when her eyes are closed in sleep.

But leave it to the *pheasant hen* to ferret out a secret. Overhearing *Chantecler's* conversation with the *woodpecker,* she is furious. "I will not let the sun defraud me of my love," she cries. But *Chantecler* replies, "There is no great love outside of the shadow of the ideal." She makes use of her beauty and charm to win him from the sun. She embraces him and pleads, "Come to my soft bosom. Why need you bother about the sun?"

Chantecler hears the nightingale and, like all great artists, he recognizes her wonderful voice, her inspiring powers compared with which his own must seem hard and crude. Suddenly a shot is heard, and the little bird falls dead to the ground. *Chantecler* is heart-broken. And as he mourns the sweet singer, the dawn begins to break. The *pheasant hen* covers him with her wing, to keep him from seeing the sun rise, and then mocks him because the sun has risen without his crowing. The shock is terrible to poor *Chantecler,* yet in his desperation he gives one tremendous cock-a-doodle-do.

"Why are you crowing?" the hen asks.

"As a warning to myself, for thrice have I denied the thing I love."

Chantecler is in despair. But now he hears another Nightingale, more silvery and beautiful than the first. "Learn, comrade, this sorrowful and reassuring fact, that no one, Cock of the morning or evening nightingale, has quite the song of his dreams."

A wonderful message, for there must always be "in the soul a faith so faithful that it comes back even after it has been slain." It is vital to understand that it is rather the consciousness that though we cannot wake the dawn, we must prepare the people to greet the rising sun.

BRIEUX

DAMAGED GOODS

In the preface to the English edition of "Damaged Goods," George Bernard Shaw relates a story concerning Lord Melbourne, in the early days of Queen Victoria. When the cabinet meeting threatened to break up in confusion, Lord Melbourne put his back to the door and said: "Gentlemen, we can tell the house the truth or we can tell it a lie. I don't give a damn which it is. All I insist on is that we shall all tell the same lie, and you shall not leave the room until you have settled what it is to be."

This seems to characterize the position of our middle-class morality to-day. Whether a thing be right or wrong, we are all to express the same opinion on the subject. All must agree on the same lie, and the lie upon which all agree, more than on any other, is the lie of purity, which must be kept up at all costs.

How slow our moralists move is best proved by the fact that although the great scientist Neisser had discovered, as far back as 1879, that supposedly insignificant venereal afflictions are due to a malignant micro-organism often disastrous not only to the immediate victim, but also to those who come in touch with him, the subject is still largely tabooed and must not be discussed.

To be sure, there is a small contingent of men and women who realize the necessity of a frank discussion of the very important matter of venereal disease. But unfortunately they are attempting to drive out the devil with fire. They are enlightening the public as to the gravity of gonorrhea and syphilis, but are implanting an evil by no means less harmful, namely, the element of fear. The result often is that the victims who contract an infection are as little capable of taking care of themselves now as in the past when they knew little about the subject.

Brieux is among the few who treats the question in a frank manner, showing that the most dangerous phase of venereal disease is ignorance and fear, and that if treated openly and intelligently, it is perfectly curable. Brieux also emphasizes the importance of kindness and consideration for those who contract the affliction, since it has nothing to do with what is commonly called evil, immorality, or impurity.

Therein lies the superiority of "Damaged Goods" to most scientific treatises. Without lacking logic and clarity, it has greater humanity and warmth.

But "Damaged Goods" contains more than an exposé of venereal disease. It touches upon the whole of our social life. It points out the cold-blooded indifference of the rich toward those who do not belong to their class, to the poor, the workers, the disinherited whom they sacrifice without the slightest compunction on the altar of their own comforts. Moreover, the play also treats of the contemptible attitude towards love not backed by property or legal sanction. In short, it uncovers and exposes not only sexual disease but that which is even more terrible—our social disease, our social syphilis.

George Dupont, the son of wealthy people, is informed by a specialist that he has contracted a venereal disease of a most serious nature; but that with patience and time he will be cured. *Dupont* is crushed by the news, and decides to blow out his brains. His only regret is that he cannot in the least account for his trouble.

George. I'm not a rake, Doctor. My life might be held up as an example to all young men. I assure you, no one could possibly be more prudent, no one. See here; supposing I told you that in all my life I have only had two mistresses, what would you say to that?

Doctor. That would have been enough to bring you here.

George. No, Doctor. Not one of those two. No one in the world has dreaded this so much as I have; no one has taken such infinite precautions to avoid it. My first mistress was the wife of my best friend. I chose her on account of him; and him, not because I cared most for him, but because I knew he was a man of the most rigid morals, who watched his wife jealously and didn't let her go about forming imprudent connections. As for her, I kept her in absolute terror of this disease. I told her that almost all men were taken with it, so that she mightn't dream of being false to me. My friend died in my arms. That was the only thing that could have separated me from her. Then I took up with a young seamstress. . . . Well, this was a decent girl with a family in needy circumstances to support. Her grandmother was an invalid, and there was an ailing father and three little brothers. It was by my means that they all lived. . . . I told her and I let the others know that if she played me false I should leave her at once. So then they all watched her for me. It became a regular thing that I should spend Sunday with them, and in that sort of way I was able to give her a lift up. Church-going was a respectable kind of outing for her. I rented a pew for them and her mother used to go with her to church; they liked seeing their name engraved on the card. She never left the house alone. Three months ago, when the question of my marriage came up, I had to leave her.

Doctor. You were very happy, why did you want to change?

George. I wanted to settle down. My father was a notary, and before his death he expressed a wish that I should marry my cousin. It was a good match; her dowry will help to get me a practice. Besides, I simply adore her. She's fond of me, too. I had everything one could want to make my life happy. And then a lot of idiots must give me a farewell dinner and make me gad about with them. See what has come of it! I haven't any luck, I've never had any luck! I know fellows who lead the most racketty life: nothing happens to them, the beasts! But I—for a wretched lark—what is there left for a leper like me? My future is ruined, my whole life poisoned. Well then, isn't it better for me to clear out of it? Anyway, I shan't suffer any more. You see now, no one could be more wretched than I am.

The doctor explains to him that there is no need for despair, but that he must postpone his marriage if he does not wish to ruin his wife and possibly make her sterile for life. It is imperative especially because of the offspring, which is certain to be syphilitic.

Doctor. Twenty cases identical with yours have been carefully observed—from the beginning to the end. Nineteen times—you hear, nineteen times in twenty—the woman was contaminated by her husband. You think that the danger is negligible: you think you have the right to let your wife take her chance, as you said, of being one of the exceptions for which we can do nothing! Very well then; then you shall know what you are doing. You shall know what sort of a disease it is that your wife will have five chances per cent. of contracting without so much as having her leave asked. . . . But there is not only your wife,—there are her children, your children, whom you may contaminate, too. It is in the name of those innocent little ones that I appeal to you; it is the future of the race that I am defending.

But *George Dupont* will not postpone the marriage for several years. He would have to give an explanation, break his word, and lose his inheritance, —things infinitely more important than any consideration for the girl he "adores" or for their children, should they have any. In short, he is actuated by the morality of the bourgeoisie: the silly conception of honor, the dread of public opinion and, above all, the greed for property.

The second act is laid at the home of *George Dupont*. *George* and his wife *Henriette* are childishly happy, except for the regret that their marriage could not have taken place six months earlier because poor George had been declared consumptive. How stupid of doctors to suspect the healthy strong *George Dupont* of consumption! But, then, "all doctors are stupid." But now that they are together, nothing shall part them in their great happiness, and especially in their great love for their baby. True, a little cloud obscures their sunny horizon. The baby is not very strong; but with the care and devotion of the grandmother, out in the country air, it is sure to recover.

The grandmother unexpectedly arrives, announcing that she has brought the baby back to town: it is very ill and she has consulted a specialist who has promised to come at once to examine the child. Presently the doctor arrives. He insists that the wet nurse be dismissed immediately, as the child would infect her and she in return would infect her own husband and baby. *Madame Dupont* is scandalized. What, leave her precious grandchild! Rob him of the milk he needs!

Mme. Dupont. If there is one way to save its life, it is to give it every possible attention, and you want me to treat it in a way that you doctors condemn even for healthy children. You think I will let her die like that! Oh, I shall take good care she does not! Neglect the one single thing that can save her! It would be criminal! As for the nurse, we will indemnify her. We will do everything in our power, everything but that.

Doctor. This is not the first time I have found myself in this situation, and I must begin by telling you that parents who have refused to be guided by my advice have invariably repented of it most bitterly.... You propose to profit by her ignorance and her poverty. Besides, she could obtain the assistance of the court.... You can convince yourself. In one or two cases the parents have been ordered to pay a yearly pension to the nurse; in the others sums of money varying from three to eight thousand francs.

Mme. Dupont. If we had to fight an action, we should retain the very best lawyer on our side. Thank heaven we are rich enough. No doubt he would make it appear doubtful whether the child hadn't caught this disease from the nurse, rather than the nurse from the child.

Indeed, what matters a peasant woman! They are so numerous. In vain the doctor tries to convince *Mme. Dupont* that it is not a question of money. It is a question of humanity, of decency; he would not and could not be a party to such a crime.

After the doctor leaves to examine the child, *Mme. Dupont* and her worthy son clinch the bargain with the unsuspecting and ignorant servant. They tell her that the baby has a cold which it might communicate to her. The poor peasant girl had lived in the cold all her life, and as she justly says: "We of the country are not as delicate as the Parisian ladies." She realizes that a thousand francs would mean a great fortune to her, and that it would help her people to pay the mortgage and become independent. She consents to stay and signs away her health.

The doctor returns with the dreaded news that the child has congenital syphilis. He informs them that with care and patience the child might be cured, but that it will have to be put on bottle milk, because otherwise it would be disastrous to the nurse. When he is told that the nurse has consented to remain, he grows indignant, declaring:

"You must not ask me to sacrifice the health of a young and strong woman to that of a sickly infant. I will be no party to giving this woman a disease that would embitter the lives of her whole family, and almost certainly render her sterile. Besides, I cannot even do it from a legal standpoint . . . *If you do not consent to have the child fed by hand, I shall either speak to the nurse or give up the case.*"

But there is no need for the doctor to interfere. Fortunately for the servant, she discovers the miserable transaction. She learns from the butler the real condition of the child, and announces to the Duponts that she must refuse to stay. "I know your brat isn't going to live. I know it's rotten through and through because its father's got a beastly disease that he caught from some woman of the streets."

At this terrible moment the unsuspecting, light-headed and light-hearted mother, *Henriette,* arrives. She overhears the horrible news and falls screaming to the floor.

The last act takes place in the hospital—the refuge of the unfortunate victims of poverty, ignorance and false morality. *M. Loche,* the Deputy, is announced. The doctor is overjoyed because he believes that the representative of the people comes to inform himself of the causes of the widespread misery. But he is mistaken. *M. Loche* is the father-in-law of *George Dupont.* He wants to secure the signature of the doctor as evidence in the divorce sought by his daughter.

Doctor. I regret that I am unable to furnish you with such a certificate. . . . The rule of professional secrecy is absolute. And I may add that even were I free, I should refuse your request. I should regret having helped you to obtain a divorce. It would be in your daughter's own interest that I should refuse. You ask me for a certificate in order to prove to the court that your son-in-law has contracted syphilis? You do not consider that in doing so you will publicly acknowledge that your daughter has been exposed to the infection. Do you suppose that after that your daughter is likely to find a second husband? ... Do you think that this poor little thing has not been unlucky enough in her start in life? She has been blighted physically. You wish besides indelibly to stamp her with the legal proof of congenital syphilis.

Loche. Then what am I to do?

Doctor. Forgive. ... When the marriage was proposed you doubtless made inquiries concerning your future son-in-law's income; you investigated his securities; you satisfied yourself as to his character. You only omitted one point, but it was the most important of all: you made no inquiries concerning his health.

Loche. No, I did not do that. It is not the custom. ... I think a law should be passed.

Doctor. No, no! We want no new laws. There are too many already. All that is needed is for people to understand the nature of this disease rather better. It would soon become the custom for a man who proposed for a girl's hand to add to the other things for which he is asked a medical statement of bodily fitness, which would make it certain that he did not bring this plague into the family with him. ... Well, there is one last argument which, since I must, I will put to you. Are you yourself without sin, that you are so relentless to others?

Loche. I have never had any shameful disease, sir.

Doctor. I was not asking you that. I was asking you if you had never exposed yourself to catching one. Ah, you see! Then it is not virtue that has saved you; it is luck. Few things exasperate me more than that term "shameful disease," which you used just now. This disease is like all other diseases: it is one of our afflictions. There is no shame in being wretched—even if one deserves to be so. Come, come, let us have a little plain speaking! I should like to know how many of these rigid moralists, who are so shocked with their middle-class prudery, that they dare not mention the name syphilis, or when they bring themselves to speak of it do so with expressions of every sort of disgust, and treat its victims as criminals, have never run the risk of contracting it themselves? It is those alone who have the right to talk. How many do you think there are? Four out of a thousand? Well, leave those four aside: between all the rest and those who catch the disease there is no difference but chance, and by heavens, those who escape won't get much sympathy from me: the others at least have paid their fine of suffering and remorse, while they have gone scot free! Let's have done, if you please, once for all with this sort of hypocrisy.

The doctor, who is not only a sincere scientist but also a humanitarian, realizes that as things are today no one is exempt from the possibility of contracting an infection; that those who are responsible for the spread of the disease are they who constantly excuse themselves with the inane "I did not know," as if ignorance were not the crime of all crimes. The doctor demonstrates to *M. Loche* a number of cases under his observation, all of them the result of ignorance and of poverty.

There is, for instance, the woman whose husband died of the disease. He "didn't know"; so he infected her. She, on the other hand, is poor and cannot afford the treatment she needs. A private physician is beyond her means, and she has too much pride to stand the indignities heaped upon the poor who are at the mercy of dispensaries and charity. Therefore she neglects her disease and perhaps is unconsciously instrumental in infecting others.

Then there is the man whose young son has contracted the disease. His father "didn't know," and therefore he did not inform his son, as a result of which the boy became half paralyzed.

Man. We are small trades-people; we have regularly bled ourselves in order to send him to college, and now—I only wish the same thing mayn't happen to others. It was at the very college gates that my poor boy was got hold of by one of these women. Is it right, sir, that that should be allowed? Aren't there enough police to prevent children of fifteen from being seduced like that? I ask, is it right?

The poor man, in his ignorance, did not know that "these women" are the most victimized, as demonstrated by the doctor himself in the case of the poor girl of the street. She was both ignorant and innocent when she found a place as domestic servant and was seduced by her master. Then she was kicked out into the street, and in her endless search for work found every door closed in her face. She was compelled to stifle her feeling of motherhood, to send her baby to a foundling asylum, and finally, in order to exist, become a street-walker. If in return she infected the men who came to her, including her erstwhile seducer, she was only paying back in a small measure what society had done to her,—the injury, the bitterness, the misery and tears heaped upon her by a cruel and self-satisfied world.

It is to be expected that a political representative of the people like *Loche* should suggest the same stereotyped measures as his predecessors: legal enactments, prosecution, imprisonment. But the doctor, a real social student, knows that "the true remedy lies in a change of our ways."

Doctor. Syphilis must cease to be treated like a mysterious evil, the very name of which cannot be pronounced. . . . People ought to be taught that there is nothing immoral in the act that reproduces life by means of love. But for the benefit of our children we organize round about it a gigantic conspiracy of silence. A respectable man will take his son and daughter to one of these grand music halls, where they will hear things of the most loathsome description; but he won't let them hear a word spoken seriously on the subject of the great act of love. The mystery and humbug in which physical facts are enveloped ought to be swept away and young men be given some pride in the creative power with which each one of us is endowed.

In other words, what we need is more general enlightenment, greater frankness and, above all, different social and economic conditions. The revolutionary significance of "Damaged Goods" consists in the lesson that not syphilis but the causes that lead to it are the terrible curse of society. Those who rant against syphilis and clamor for more laws, for marriage certificates, for registration and segregation, do not touch even the surface of the evil. Brieux is among the very few modern dramatists who go to the bottom of this question by insisting on a complete social and economic change, which alone can free us from the scourge of syphilis and other social plagues.

MATERNITY

Motherhood to-day is on the lips of every penny-a-liner, every social patch-worker and political climber. It is so much prated about that one is led to believe that motherhood, in its present condition, is a force for good. It therefore required a free spirit combined with great dramatic power to tear the mask off the lying face of motherhood, that we may see that, whatever its possibilities in a free future, motherhood is today a sickly tree setting forth diseased branches. For its sake thousands of women are being sacrificed and children sent into a cold and barren world without the slightest provision for their physical and mental needs. It was left to Brieux to inscribe with letters of fire the crying shame of the motherhood of to-day.

Brignac, a provincial lawyer and an unscrupulous climber for political success, represents the typical pillar of society. He believes implicitly in the supremacy of God over the destiny of man. He swears by the State and the army, and cringes before the power of money. Naturally he is the champion of large families as essential to the welfare of society, and of motherhood, as the most sacred and sole function of woman.

He is the father of three children, all of whom are in a precarious condition. He resents the idea that society ought to take care of the children already in existence, rather than continue indiscriminately breeding more. *Brignac* himself wants more children. In vain his wife *Lucie,* weakened by repeated pregnancies, pleads with him for a respite.

Lucie. Listen, Julien, since we are talking about this. I wanted to tell you—I haven't had much leisure since our marriage. We have not been able to take advantage of a single one of your holidays. I really have a right to a little rest. . . . Consider, we have not had any time to know one another, or to love one another. Besides, remember that we already have to find dowries for three girls.

Brignac. I tell you this is going to be a boy.

Lucie. A boy is expensive.

Brignac. We are going to be rich.

Lucie. How?

Brignac. Luck may come in several ways. I may stay in the civil service and get promoted quickly. I may go back to the bar. . . . I am certain we shall be rich. After all, it's not much good your saying no, if I say yes.

Lucie. Evidently. My consent was asked for before I was given a husband, but my consent is not asked for before I am given a child. . . . This is slavery—yes, *slavery.* After all you are disposing of my health, my sufferings, my life—of a year of my existence, calmly, without consulting me.

Brignac. Do I do it out of selfishness? Do you suppose I am not a most unhappy husband all the time I have a future mother at my side instead of a loving wife? . . . A father is a man all the same.

Lucie. Rubbish! You evidently take me for a fool. I know what you do at those times. . . . Don't deny it. You must see that I know all about it. . . . Do you want me to tell you the name of the person you go to see over at Villeneuve, while I am nursing or "a future mother," as you call it? We had better say no more about it.

Brignac goes off to his political meeting to proclaim to his constituency the sacredness of motherhood,—the deepest and highest function of woman.

Lucie has a younger sister, *Annette,* a girl of eighteen. Their parents being dead, *Lucie* takes the place of the mother. She is passionately fond of her little sister and makes it her purpose to keep the girl sheltered and protected from the outside world. *Annette* arrives and announces with great enthusiasm that the son of the wealthy Bernins has declared his love and asked her to marry him, and that his mother, *Mme. Bernin,* is coming to talk the matter over with *Lucie.*

Mme. Bernin does arrive, but not for the purpose poor *Annette* had hoped. Rather it is to tell *Lucie* that her son cannot marry the girl. Oh, not because she isn't beautiful, pure or attractive. Indeed not! *Mme. Bernin* herself says that her son could not wish for a more suitable match. But, then, she has no money, and her son must succeed in the world. He must acquire social standing and position; that cannot be had without money. When *Lucie* pleads with her that after all the Bernins themselves had begun at the bottom, and that it did not prevent their being happy, *Mme. Bernin* replies:

No, no; we are not happy, because we have worn ourselves out hunting after happiness. We wanted to "get on," and we got on. But what a price we paid for it! First, when we were both earning wages, our life was one long drudgery of petty economy and meanness. When we set up on our own account, we lived in an atmosphere of trickery, of enmity, of lying; flattering the customers, and always in terror of bankruptcy. Oh, I know the road to fortune! It means tears, lies, envy, hate; one suffers—and one makes other people suffer. I have had to go through it: my children shan't. We've only had two children: we meant only to have one. Having two we had to be doubly hard upon ourselves. Instead of a husband and wife helping one another, we have been partners spying upon one another; calling one another to account for every little expenditure or stupidity; and on our very pillows disputing about our business. That's how we got rich; and now we can't enjoy our money because we don't know how to use it; and we aren't happy because our old age is made bitter by the memories and the rancor left by the old bad days; because we have suffered too much and hated too much. My children shall not go through this. I endured it that they might be spared.

Learning the price *Mme. Bernin* has paid for her wealth, we need not blame her for turning a deaf ear to the entreaties of *Lucie* in behalf of her sister. Neither can *Lucie* be held responsible for her stupidity in keeping her sister in ignorance until she was incapable of protecting herself when the occasion demanded. Poor *Annette,* one of the many offered up to the insatiable monster of ignorance and social convention!

When *Annette* is informed of the result of *Mme. Bernin's* visit, the girl grows hysterical, and *Lucie* learns that her little sister is about to become a mother. Under the pretext of love and marriage young, pampered *Jaques Bernin* has taken advantage of the girl's inexperience and innocence. In her despair *Annette* rushes out in search of her lover, only to be repelled by him in a vulgar and cruel manner. She then attempts suicide by trying to throw herself under the train which is to carry off her worthless seducer. She is rescued by the faithful nurse *Catherine,* and brought back to her anxious sister *Lucie. Annette,* in great excitement, relates:

Annette. You'll never guess what he said. He got angry, and he began to abuse me. He said he guessed what I was up to; that I wanted to make a scandal to force him to marry me—oh, he spared me nothing—to force him to marry me because he was rich. And when that made me furious, he threatened to call the police! I ought to have left him, run away, come home, oughtn't I? But I couldn't believe it of him all at once, like that! And I couldn't go away while I had any hope.... As long as I was holding to his arm it was as if I was engaged. When he was gone I should only be a miserable ruined girl, like dozens of others.... My life was at stake: and to save myself I went down into the very lowest depths of vileness and cowardice. I cried, I implored. I lost all shame. ... What he said then I cannot tell you—not even you—it was too much—too much—I did not understand at first. It was only afterwards, coming back, going over all his words, that I made out what he meant.... Then he rushed to the train, and jumped into a carriage, and almost crushed my fingers in the door; and he went and hid behind his mother, and she threatened, too, to have me arrested.... I wish I was dead! Lucie, dear, I don't want to go through all that's coming—I am too little—I am too weak, I'm too young to bear it. Really, I haven't the strength.

But *Lucie* has faith in her husband. In all the years of their married life she has heard him proclaim from the very housetops that motherhood is the most sacred function of woman; that the State needs large numbers; that commerce and the army require an increase of the population, and "the government commands you to further this end to the best of your ability, each one of you in his own commune." She has heard her husband repeat, over and over again, that the woman who refuses to abide by the command of God and the laws to become a mother is immoral, is criminal. Surely he would understand the tragedy of *Annette,* who had been placed in this condition not through her own fault but because she had been confiding and trusting in the promise of the man. Surely *Brignac* would come to the rescue of *Annette;* would help and comfort her in her trying and difficult moment. But *Lucie,* like many wives, does not know her husband; she does not know that a man who is so hide-bound by statutes and codes cannot have human compassion, and that he will not stand by the little girl who has committed the "unpardonable sin." *Lucie* does not know, but she is soon to learn the truth.

Lucie. I tell you Annette is the victim of this wretch. If you are going to do nothing but insult her, we had better stop discussing the matter.

Brignac. I am in a nice fix now! There is nothing left for us but to pack our trunks and be off. I am done for. Ruined! Smashed! I tell you if she was caught red handed stealing, the wreck wouldn't be more complete. . . . We must make some excuse. We will invent an aunt or cousin who has invited her to stay. I will find a decent house for her in Paris to go to. She'll be all right there. When the time comes she can put the child out to nurse in the country, and come back to us.

Lucie. You seriously propose to send that poor child to Paris, where she doesn't know a soul?

Brignac. What do you mean by that? I will go to Paris myself, if necessary. There are special boarding houses: very respectable ones. I'll inquire: of course without letting out that it is for anyone I know. And I'll pay what is necessary. What more can you want?

Lucie. Just when the child is most in need of every care, you propose to send her off alone; alone, do you understand, alone! To tear her away from here, put her into a train, and send her off to Paris, like a sick animal you want to get rid of. If I consented to that I should feel that I was as bad as the man who seduced her. Be honest, Julien: remember it is in our interest you propose to sacrifice her. We shall gain peace and quiet at the price of her loneliness and despair. To save our-selves—serious troubles, I admit—we are to abandon this child to strangers . . . away from all love and care and comfort, without a friend to put kind arms around her and let her sob her grief away. I implore you, Julien, I entreat you, for our children's sake, don't keep me from her, don't ask me to do this shameful thing.

Brignac. There would have been no question of misery if she had behaved herself.

Lucie. She is this man's victim! But she won't go. You'll have to drive her out as you drove out the servant . . . And then—after that—she is to let her child go; to stifle her strongest instinct; to silence the cry of love that consoles us all for the tortures we have to go through; to turn away her eyes and say, "Take him away, I don't want him." And at that price she is to be forgiven for another person's crime. . . . Then that is Society's welcome to the new born child?

Brignac. To the child born outside of marriage, yes. If it wasn't for that, there would soon be nothing but illegitimate births. It is to preserve the family that society condemns the natural child.

Lucie. You say you want a larger number of births, and at the same time you say to women: "No motherhood without marriage, and no marriage without money." As long as you've not changed that, all your circulars will be met with shouts of derision—half from hate, half from pity. . . . If you drive Annette out, I shall go with her.

Lucie and *Annette* go out into the world. As middle-class girls they have been taught a little of everything and not much of anything. They try all kinds of work to enable them to make a living, but though they toil hard and long hours, they barely earn enough for a meager existence. As long as *Annette's* condition is not noticeable, life is bearable; but soon everybody remarks her state. She and *Lucie* are driven from place to place. In her despair *Annette* does what many girls in her position have done before her and will do after her so long as the Brignacs and their morality are dominant. She visits a midwife, and one more victim is added to the large number slaughtered upon the altar of morality.

The last act is in the court room. *Mme. Thomas,* the midwife, is on trial for criminal abortion. With her are a number of women whose names have been found on her register.

Bit by bit we learn the whole tragedy of each of the defendants; we see all the sordidness of poverty, the inability to procure the bare necessities of life, and the dread of the unwelcome child.

A schoolmistress, although earning a few hundred francs, and living with her husband, is compelled to have an abortion performed because another child would mean hunger for all of them.

Schoolmistress. We just managed to get along by being most careful; and several times we cut down expenses it did not seem possible to cut down. A third child coming upset everything. We couldn't have lived. We should have all starved. Besides, the inspectors and directresses don't like us to have many children, especially if we nurse them ourselves. They told me to hide myself when I was suckling the last one. I only had ten minutes to do it in, at the recreation, at ten o'clock and at two o'clock; and when my mother brought baby to me I had to shut myself up with him in a dark closet.

The couple *Tupin* stand before the bar to defend themselves against the charge of criminal abortion. *Tupin* has been out of work for a long time and is driven by misery to drink. He is known to the police as a disreputable character. One of his sons is serving a sentence for theft, and a daughter is a woman of the streets. But *Tupin* is a thinking man. He proves that his earnings at best are not enough to supply the needs of an already large family. The daily nourishment of five children consists of a four-pound loaf, soup of vegetables and dripping, and a stew which costs 90 centimes. Total, 3f. 75c. This is the expenditure of the father: Return ticket for tram, 30c. Tobacco, 15c. Dinner, 1f.25c. The rent, 300f. Clothing for the whole family, and boots: 16 pairs of boots for the children at 4f. 50c each, 4 for the parents at 8f., total again 300f. Total for the year, 2,600f. *Tupin,* who is an exceptional workman, earns 160f. a month, that is to say, 2,100f. a year. There is therefore an annual deficit of 500f., provided *Tupin* keeps at work all the time, which never happens in the life of a workingman. Under such circumstances no one need be surprised that one of his children is imprisoned for theft, and the other is walking the streets, while *Tupin* himself is driven to drink.

Tupin. When we began to get short in the house, my wife and I started to quarrel. Every time a child came we were mad at making it worse for the others. And so. . . . I ended up in the saloon. It's warm there, and you can't hear the children crying nor the mother complaining. And besides, when you have drink in you, you forget. . . . And that's how we got poorer and poorer. My fault, if you like. . . . Our last child was a cripple. He was born in starvation, and his mother was worn out. And they nursed him, and they nursed him, and they nursed him. They did not leave him a minute. They made him live in spite of himself. And they let the other children—the strong ones—go to the bad. With half the money and the fuss they wasted on the cripple, they could have made fine fellows of all the others.

Mme. Tupin. I have to add that all this is not my fault. My husband and I worked like beasts; we did without every kind of pleasure to try and bring up our children. If we had wanted to slave more, I declare to you we couldn't have done it. And now that we have given our lives for them, the oldest is in hospital, ruined and done for because he worked in "a dangerous trade" as they call it. . . . There are too many people in the world. . . . My little girl had to choose between starvation and the street. . . . I'm only a poor woman, and I know what it means to have nothing to eat, so I forgave her.

Thus *Mme. Tupin* also understands that it is a crime to add one more victim to those who are born ill and for whom society has no place.

Then *Lucie* faces the court,—*Lucie* who loved her sister too well, and who, driven by the same conditions that killed *Annette,* has also been compelled to undergo an abortion rather than have a fourth child by the man she did not love any more. Like the *Schoolmistress* and the *Tupins,* she is dragged before the bar of justice to explain her crime, while her husband, who had forced both *Annette* and *Lucie* out of the house, has meanwhile risen to a high position as a supporter of the State with his favorite slogan, "Motherhood is the highest function of woman."

Finally the midwife *Thomas* is called upon for her defense.

Thomas. A girl came to me one day; she was a servant. She had been seduced by her master. I refused to do what she asked me to do: she went and drowned herself. Another I refused to help was brought up before you here for infanticide. Then when the others came, I said, "Yes." I have prevented many a suicide and many a crime.

It is not likely the the venerable judge, the State's attorney or the gentlemen of the jury can see in *Mme. Thomas* a greater benefactress to society than they; any more than they can grasp the deep importance of the concluding words of the counsel for the defense in this great social tragedy.

Counsel for the Defense. Their crime is not an individual crime; it is a social crime. . . . It is *not* a crime against nature. It is a revolt against nature. And with all the warmth of a heart melted by pity, with all the indignation of my outraged reason, I look for that glorious hour of liberation when some master mind shall discover for us the means of having only the children we need and desire, release forever from the prison of hypocrisy and absolve us from the profanation of love. That would indeed be a conquest of nature—savage nature—which pours out life with culpable profusion, and sees it disappear with indifference.

Surely there can be no doubt as to the revolutionary significance of "Maternity": the demand that woman must be given means to prevent conception of undesired and unloved children; that she must become free and strong to choose the father of her child and to decide the number of children she is to bring into the world, and under what conditions. That is the only kind of motherhood which can endure.

THE ENGLISH DRAMA

GEORGE BERNARD SHAW

"I am not an ordinary playwright in general practice. I am a specialist in immoral and heretical plays. My reputation has been gained by my persistent struggle to force the public to reconsider its morals. In particular, I regard much current morality as to economic and sexual relations as disastrously wrong; and I regard certain doctrines of the Christian religion as understood in England to-day with abhorrence. I write plays with the deliberate object of converting the nation to my opinions in these matters."

This confession of faith should leave no doubt as to the place of George Bernard Shaw in modern dramatic art. Yet, strange to say, he is among the most doubted of his time. That is partly due to the fact that humor generally serves merely to amuse, touching only the lighter side of life. But there is a kind of humor that fills laughter with tears, a humor that eats into the soul like acid, leaving marks often deeper than those made by the tragic form.

There is another reason why Shaw's sincerity is regarded lightly: it is to be found in the difference of his scope as propagandist and as artist. As the propagandist Shaw is limited, dogmatic, and set. Indeed, the most zealous Puritan could not be more antagonistic to social theories differing from his own. But the artist, if he is sincere at all, must go to life as the source of his inspiration, and life is beyond dogmas, beyond the House of Commons, beyond even the "eternal and irrevocable law" of the materialistic conception of history. If, then, the Socialist propagandist Shaw is often lost in the artist Shaw, it is not because he lacks sincerity, but because life will not be curtailed.

It may be contended that Shaw is much more the propagandist than the artist because he paints in loud colors. But that is rather because of the indolence of the human mind, especially of the Anglo-Saxon mind, which has settled down snugly to the self-satisfied notion of its purity, justice, and charity, so that naught but the strongest current of light will make it wince. In "Mrs. Warren's Profession" and "Major Barbara," George Bernard Shaw has accomplished even more. He has pulled off the mask of purity and Christian kindness that we may see their hidden viciousness at work.

MRS. WARREN'S PROFESSION

Mrs. Warren is engaged in a profession which has existed through all the ages. It was at home in Egypt, played an important rôle in Greece and Rome, formed one of the influential guilds in the Middle Ages, and has been one of the main sources of income for the Christian Church.

But it was left to modern times to make of Mrs. Warren's profession a tremendous social factor, ministering to the needs of man in every station of life, from the brownstone mansion to the hovel, from the highest official to the poorest drag.

Time was when the Mrs. Warrens were looked upon as possessed by the devil,—lewd, depraved creatures who would not, even if they had the choice, engage in any other profession, because they are vicious at heart, and should therefore be held up to condemnation and obloquy. And while we continue to drive them from pillar to post, while we still punish them as criminals and deny them the simplest humanities one gives even to the dumb beast, the light turned on this subject by men like George Bernard Shaw has helped to expose the lie of inherent evil tendencies and natural depravity. Instead we learn:

Mrs. Warren. Do you think I did what I did because I liked it, or thought it right, or wouldn't rather have gone to college and been a lady if I'd had the chance? . . . Oh, it's easy to talk, very easy, isn't it? Here!—Would you like to know what my circumstances were? D'you know what your gran'mother was? No, you don't. I do. She called herself a widow and had a fried-fish shop down by the Mint, and kept herself and four daughters out of it. Two of us were sisters: that was me and Liz; and we were both good looking and well made. I suppose our father was a well fed man: mother pretended he was a gentleman; but I don't know. The other two were only half sisters—undersized, ugly, starved, hard working, honest poor creatures: Liz and I would have half murdered them if mother hadn't half murdered us to keep our hands off them. They were the respectable ones. Well, what did they get by their respectability? I'll tell you. One of them worked in a whitelead factory twelve hours a day for nine shillings a week until she died of lead poisoning. She only expected to get her hands a little paralyzed; but she died. The other was always held up to us as a model because she married a Government laborer in the Deptford victualling yard, and kept his room and the three children neat and tidy on eighteen shillings a week—until he took to drink. That was worth being respectable for, wasn't it?

Vivie. Did you and your sister think so?

Mrs. Warren. Liz didn't, I can tell you; she had more spirit. We both went to a Church School—that was part of the lady-like airs we gave ourselves to be superior to the children that knew nothing and went nowhere—and we stayed there until Liz went out one night and never came back. I knew the schoolmistress thought I'd soon follow her example; for the clergyman was always warning me that Lizzie'd end by jumping off Waterloo Bridge. Poor fool: that was all that he knew about it! But I was more afraid of the whitelead factory than I was of the river; and so would you have been in my place. That clergyman got me a situation as a scullery maid in a temperance restaurant where they sent out for anything you liked. Then I was waitress; and then I went to the bar at Waterloo Station—fourteen hours a day serving drinks and washing glasses for four shillings a week and my board. That was considered a great promotion for me. Well, one cold, wretched night, when I was so tired I could hardly keep myself awake, who should come up for a half of Scotch but Lizzie, in a long fur cloak, elegant and comfortable, with a lot of sovereigns in her purse.

Vivie. My aunt Lizzie?

Mrs. Warren. Yes. . . . She's living down at Winchester, now, close to the cathedral, one of the most respectable ladies there—chaperones girls at the country ball, if you please. No river for Liz, thank you! You remind me of Liz a little: she was a first-rate business woman—saved money from the beginning—never let herself look too like what she was—never lost her head or threw away a chance. When she saw I'd grown up good-looking she said to me across the bar: "What are you doing there, you little fool? Wearing out your health and your appearance for other people's profit!" Liz was saving money then to take a house for herself in Brussels: and she thought we two could save faster than one. So she lent me some money and gave me a start; and I saved steadily and first paid her back, and then went into business with her as her partner. Why shouldn't I have done it? The house in Brussels was real high class—a much better place for a woman to be in than the factory where Anne Jane got poisoned. None of our girls were ever treated as I was treated in the scullery of that temperance place, or at the Waterloo bar, or at home. Would you have had me stay in them and become a worn-out old drudge before I was forty? . . . Yes, saving money. But where can a woman get the money to save in any other business? Could you save out of four shillings a week and keep yourself dressed as well? Not you. Of course, if you're a plain woman and can't earn anything more: or if you have a turn for music, or the stage, or newspaper writing: that's different. But neither Liz nor I had any turn for such things: all we had was our appearance and our turn for pleasing men. Do you think we were such fools as to let other people trade in our good looks by employing us as shop-girls, or barmaids, or waitresses, when we could trade in them ourselves and get all the profits instead of starvation wages? Not likely. . . . Everybody dislikes having to work and make money; but they have to do it all the same. I'm sure I've often pitied a poor girl, tired out and in low spirits, having to try to please some man that she doesn't care two straws for—some half-drunken fool that thinks he's making himself agreeable when he's teasing and worrying and disgusting a woman so that hardly any money could pay her for putting up with it. But she has to bear with disagreeables and take the rough with the smooth, just like a nurse in a hospital or anyone else. It's not work that any woman would do for pleasure, goodness knows; though to hear the pious people talk you would suppose it was a bed of roses. Of course it's worth while to a poor girl, if she can resist temptation and is good looking and well-conducted and sensible. It's far better than any other employment open to her. I always thought that oughtn't to be. It can't be right, Vivie, that there shouldn't be better opportunities for women. I stick to that: It's wrong. But it's so, right or wrong; and a girl must make the best of it. But, of course, it's not worth while for a lady. If you took to it you'd be a fool; but I should have been a fool if I'd taken to anything else. . . . Why am I independent and able to give my daughter a first-rate education, when other women that had just as good opportunities are in the gutter? Because I always knew how to respect myself and control myself. Why is Liz looked up to in a cathedral town? The same reason. Where would we be now if we'd minded the clergyman's foolishness? Scrubbing floors for one and sixpence a day and nothing to look forward to but the workhouse infirmary. Don't you be led astray by people who don't know the world, my girl. The only way for a woman to provide for herself decently is for her to be good to some man that can afford to be good to her. If she's in his own station of life, let her make him marry her; but if she's far beneath him, she can't expect it—why should she? It wouldn't be for her own happiness. Ask any lady in London society that has daughters; and she'll tell you the same, except that I tell you straight and she'll tell you crooked. That's all the difference. . . . It's only good manners to be ashamed of it; it's expected from a woman. Women have to pretend a great deal that they don't feel. Liz used to be angry with me for plumping out the truth about it. She used to say that when every woman would learn enough from what was going on in the world before her eyes, there was no need to talk about it to her. But then Liz was such a perfect lady! She had the true instinct of it; while I was always a bit of a vulgarian. I used to be so pleased when you sent me your photographs to see that you were growing up like Liz; you've just her lady-like determined way. But I can't stand saying one thing when everyone knows I mean another. What's the use in such hypocrisy? If people arrange the world that way for women, there's no use pretending that it's arranged the other way. I never was a bit ashamed really. I consider that I had a right to be proud that we managed everything so respectably, and never had a word against us, and that the girls were so well taken care of. Some of them did very well: one of them married an ambassador. But of course now I daren't talk about such things: whatever would they think of us.

No, it is not respectable to talk about these things, because respectability cannot face the truth. Yet everybody knows that the majority of women, "if they wish to provide for themselves decently must be good to some man that can afford to be good to them." The only difference then between *Sister Liz,* the respectable girl, and *Mrs. Warren,* is hypocrisy and legal sanction. *Sister Liz* uses her money to buy back her reputation from the Church and Society. The respectable girl uses the sanction of the Church to buy a decent income legitimately, and *Mrs. Warren* plays her game without the sanction of either. Hence she is the greatest criminal in the eyes of the world. Yet *Mrs. Warren* is no less human than most other women. In fact, as far as her love for her daughter *Vivian* is concerned, she is a superior sort of mother. That her daughter may not have to face the same alternative as she,—slave in a scullery for four shillings a week—*Mrs. Warren* surrounds the girl with comfort and ease, gives her an education, and thereby establishes between her child and herself an abyss which nothing can bridge. Few respectable mothers would do as much for their daughters. However, *Mrs. Warren* remains the outcast, while all those who benefit by her profession, including even her daughter *Vivian,* move in the best circles.

Sir John Crofts, Mrs. Warren's business partner, who has invested 40,000 pounds in *Mrs. Warren's* house, drawing an income of 35 per cent. out of it in the worst years, is a recognized pillar of society and an honored member of his class. Why not!

Crofts. The fact is, it's not what would be considered exactly a high-class business in my set—the county set, you know. . . . Not that there is any mystery about it: don't think that. Of course you know by your mother's being in it that it's perfectly straight and honest. I've known her for many years; and I can say of her that she'd cut off her hands sooner than touch anything that was not what it ought to be. . . . But you see you can't mention such things in society. Once let out the word hotel and everybody says you keep a public-house. You wouldn't like people to say that of your mother, would you? That's why we're so reserved about it.... Don't turn up your nose at business, Miss Vivie: where would your Newnhams and Girtons be without it?... You wouldn't refuse the acquaintance of my mother's cousin, the Duke of Belgravia, because some of the rents he gets are earned in queer ways. You wouldn't cut the Archbishop of Canterbury, I suppose, because the Ecclesiastical Commissioners have a few publicans and sinners among their tenants? Do you remember your Crofts scholarship at Newnham? Well, that was founded by my brother the M.P. He gets his 22 per cent. out of a factory with 600 girls in it, and not one of them getting wages enough to live on. How d' ye suppose most of them manage? Ask your mother. And do you expect me to turn my back on 35 per cent. when all the rest are pocketing what they can, like sensible men? No such fool! If you're going to pick and choose your acquaintances on moral principles, you'd better clear out of this country, unless you want to cut yourself out of all decent society.... The world isn't such a bad place as the croakers make out. So long as you don't fly openly in the face of society, society doesn't ask any inconvenient questions; and it makes precious short work of the cads who do. There are no secrets better kept than the secrets that everybody guesses. In the society I can introduce you to, no lady or gentleman would so far forget themselves as to discuss my business affairs or your mother's.

Indeed, no lady or gentleman would discuss the profession of *Mrs. Warren* and her confrères. But they partake of the dividends. When the evil becomes too crying, they engage in vice crusades, and call down the wrath of the Lord and the brutality of the police upon the Mrs. Warrens and her victims. While the victimizers, the Crofts, the Canterburys, Rev. Gardner —*Vivian's* own father and pious mouthpiece of the Church—and the other patrons of *Mrs. Warren's* houses parade as the protectors of woman, the home and the family.

To-day no one of the least intelligence denies the cruelty, the injustice, the outrage of such a state of affairs, any more than it is being denied that the training of woman as a sex commodity has left her any other source of income except to sell herself to one man within marriage or to many men outside of marriage. Only bigots and inexperienced girls like *Vivian* can say that "everybody has some choice. The poorest girl alive may not be able to choose between being Queen of England or Principal of Newnham; but she can choose between rag-picking and flower-selling, according to her taste."

It is astonishing how little education and college degrees teach people. Had *Vivian* been compelled to shift for herself, she would have discovered that neither rag-picking nor flower-selling brings enough to satisfy one's "taste." It is not a question of choice, but of necessity, which is the determining factor in most people's lives.

When Shaw flung *Mrs. Warren* into the smug midst of society, even the educated Vivians knew little of the compelling force which whips thousands of women into prostitution. As to the ignorant, their minds are a mental and spiritual desert. Naturally the play caused consternation. It still continues to serve as the red rag to the social bull. "Mrs. Warren's Profession" infuriates because it goes to the bottom of our evils; because it places the accusing finger upon the sorest and most damnable spot in our social fabric—SEX as woman's only commodity in the competitive market of life. "An immoral and heretical play," indeed, of very deep social significance.

MAJOR BARBARA

"Major Barbara" is of still greater social importance, inasmuch as it points to the fact that while charity and religion are supposed to minister to the poor, both institutions derive their main revenue from the poor by the perpetuation of the evils both pretend to fight.

Major Barbara, the daughter of the world renowned cannon manufacturer *Undershaft,* has joined the Salvation Army. The latter lays claim to being the most humane religious institution, because—unlike other soul savers—it does not entirely forget the needs of the body. It also teaches that the greater the sinner the more glorious the saving. But as no one is quite as black as he is painted, it becomes necessary for those who want to be saved, and incidentally to profit by the Salvation Army, to invent sins—the blacker the better.

Rummy. What am I to do? I can't starve. Them Salvation lasses is dear girls; but the better you are the worse they likes to think you were before they rescued you. Why shouldn't they 'av' a bit o' credit, poor loves? They're worn to rags by their work. And where would they get the money to rescue us if we was to let on we're no worse than other people? You know what ladies and gentlemen are.

Price. Thievin' swine! . . . We're companions in misfortune, Rummy. . . .

Rummy. Who saved you, Mr. Price? Was it Major Barbara?

Price. No: I come here on my own. I'm goin' to be Bronterre O'Brien Price, the converted painter. I know wot they like. I'll tell 'em how I blasphemed and gambled and wopped my poor old mother—

Rummy. Used you to beat your mother?

Price. Not likely. She used to beat me. No matter: you come and listen to the converted painter, and you'll hear how she was a pious woman that taught me me prayers at 'er knee, an' how I used to come home drunk and drag her out o' bed be 'er snow-white 'airs, and lam into 'er with the poker.

Rummy. That's what's so unfair to us women. Your confessions is just as big lies as ours: you don't tell what you really done no more than us; but you men can tell your lies right out at the meetin's and be made much of for it; while the sort o' confessions we az to make 'as to be whispered to one lady at a time. It ain't right, spite of all their piety.

Price. Right! Do you suppose the Army'd be allowed if it went and did right? Not much. It combs our 'air and makes us good little blokes to be robbed and put upon. But I'll play the game as good as any of 'em. I'll see somebody struck by lightnin', or hear a voice sayin', "Snobby Price: where will you spend eternity?" I'll 'ave a time of it, I tell you.

It is inevitable that the Salvation Army, like all other religious and charitable institutions, should by its very character foster cowardice and hypocrisy as a premium securing entry into heaven.

Major Barbara, being a novice, is as ignorant of this as she is unaware of the source of the money which sustains her and the work of the Salvation Army. She consistently refuses to accept the "conscience sovereign" of *Bill Walker* for beating up a Salvation lassie. Not so *Mrs. Baines,* the Army Commissioner. She is dyed in the wool in the profession of begging and will take money from the devil himself "for the Glory of God,"—the Glory of God which consists in "taking out the anger and bitterness against the rich from the hearts of the poor," a service "gratifying and convenient for all large employers." No wonder the whisky distiller *Bodger* makes the generous contribution of 5000 pounds and *Undershaft* adds his own little mite of another 5000.

Barbara is indeed ignorant or she would not protest against a fact so notorious:

Barbara. Do you know what my father is? Have you forgotten that Lord Saxmundham is Bodger the whisky man? Do you remember how we implored the

County Council to stop him from writing Bodger's Whisky in letters of fire against the sky; so that the poor drink-ruined creatures on the embankment could not wake up from their snatches of sleep without being reminded of their deadly thirst by that wicked sky sign? Do you know that the worst thing that I have had to fight here is not the devil, but Bodger, Bodger, Bodger with his whisky, his distilleries, and his tied houses? Are you going to make our shelter another tied house for him, and ask me to keep it?

Undershaft. My dear Barbara: alcohol is a very necessary article. It heals the sick— ... It assists the doctor: that is perhaps a less questionable way of putting it. It makes life bearable to millions of people who could not endure their existence if they were quite sober. It enables Parliament to do things at eleven at night that no sane person would do at eleven in the morning.

Mrs. Baines. Barbara: Lord Saxmundham gives us the money to stop drinking—to take his own business from him.

Undershaft. I also, Mrs. Baines, may claim a little disinterestedness. Think of my business! think of the widows and orphans! the men and lads torn to pieces with shrapnel and poisoned with lyddite! the oceans of blood, not one drop of which is shed in a really just cause! the ravaged crops! the peaceful peasants forced, women and men, to till their fields under the fire of opposing armies on pain of starvation! the bad blood of the fierce cowards at home who egg on others to fight for the gratification of national vanity! All this makes money for me: I am never richer, never busier than when the papers are full of it. Well, it is your work to preach peace on earth and good will to men. Every convert you make is a vote against war. Yet I give you this money to hasten my own commercial ruin.

Barbara. Drunkenness and Murder! My God, why hast thou forsaken me?

However, *Barbara's* indignation does not last very long, any more than that of her aristocratic mother, *Lady Britomart*, who has no use for her plebeian husband except when she needs his money. Similarly *Stephen*, her son, has become converted, like *Barbara*, not to the Glory Hallelujah of the Salvation Army but to the power of money and cannon. Likewise the rest of the family, including the Greek Scholar *Cusins*, *Barbara's* suitor.

During the visit to their father's factory the Undershaft family makes several discoveries. They learn that the best modern method of accumulating a large fortune consists in organizing industries in such a manner as to make the workers content with their slavery. It's a model factory.

Undershaft. It is a spotlessly clean and beautiful hillside town. There are two chapels: a Primitive one and a sophisticated one. There's even an ethical society;

but it is not much patronized, as my men are all strongly religious. In the high explosives sheds they object to the presence of agnostics as unsafe.

The family further learns that it is not high moral precepts, patriotic love of country, or similar sentiments that are the backbone of the life of the nation. It is *Undershaft* again who enlightens them of the power of money and its rôle in dictating governmental policies, making war or peace, and shaping the destinies of man.

Undershaft. The government of your country. *I* am the government of your country: I, and Lazarus. Do you suppose that you and a half a dozen amateurs like you, sitting in a row in that foolish gabble shop, can govern Undershaft and Lazarus? No, my friend: you will do what pays *us*. You will make war when it suits *us*, and keep peace when it doesn't. You will find out that trade requires certain measures when we have decided on those measures. When I want anything to keep my dividends up, you will discover that my want is a national need. When other people want something to keep my dividends down, you will call out the police and military. And in return you shall have the support and applause of my newspapers, and the delight of imagining that you are a great statesman. Government of your country! Be off with you, my boy, and play with your caucuses and leading articles and historic parties and great leaders and burning questions and the rest of your toys. I am going back to my counting house to pay the piper and call the tune. . . . To give arms to all men who offer an honest price for them, without respect of persons or principles: to Aristocrat and Republican, to Nihilist and Tsar, to Capitalist and Socialist, to Protestant and Catholic, to burglar and policeman, to black man, white man, and yellow man, to all sorts and conditions, all nationalities, all faiths, all follies, all causes and all crimes. . . . I will take an order from a good man as cheerfully as from a bad one. If you good people prefer preaching and shirking to buying my weapons and fighting the rascals, don't blame me. I can make cannons: I cannot make courage and conviction.

That is just it. The Undershafts cannot make conviction and courage; yet both are indispensable if one is to see that, in the words of *Undershaft:*

"Cleanliness and respectability do not need justification: they justify themselves. There are millions of poor people, abject people, dirty people, ill fed, ill clothed people. They poison us morally and physically: they kill the happiness of society: they force us to do away with our own liberties and to organize unnatural cruelties for fear they should rise against us and drag us down into their abyss.

Only fools fear crime: we all fear poverty. I had rather be a thief than a pauper. I had rather be a murderer than a slave. I don't want to be either; but if you force the alternative on me, then, by Heaven, I'll choose the braver and more moral one. I hate poverty and slavery worse than any other crimes whatsoever."

Cusins, the scientist, realizes the force of *Undershaft's* argument. Long enough have the people been preached at, and intellectual power used to enslave them.

Cusins. As a teacher of Greek I gave the intellectual man weapons against the common man. I now want to give the common man weapons against the intellectual man. I love the common people. I want to arm them against the lawyer, the doctor, the priest, the literary man, the professor, the artist, and the politician, who, once in authority, are the most dangerous, disastrous, and tyrannical of all the fools, rascals, and impostors.

This thought is perhaps the most revolutionary sentiment in the whole play, in view of the fact that the people everywhere are enslaved by the awe of the lawyer, the professor, and the politician, even more than by the club and gun. It is the lawyer and the politician who poison the people with "the germ of briefs and politics," thereby unfitting them for the only effective course in the great social struggle—action, resultant from the realization that poverty and inequality never have been, never can be, preached or voted out of existence.

Undershaft. Poverty and slavery have stood up for centuries to your sermons and leading articles: they will not stand up to my machine guns. Don't preach at them; don't reason with them. Kill them.

Barbara. Killing. Is that your remedy for everything?

Undershaft. It is the final test of conviction, the only lever strong enough to overturn a social system, the only way of saying Must. Let six hundred and seventy fools loose in the street; and three policemen can scatter them. But huddle them together in a certain house in Westminster; and let them go through certain ceremonies and call themselves certain names until at last they get the courage to kill; and your six hundred and seventy fools become a government. Your pious mob fills up ballot papers and imagines it is governing its masters; but the ballot paper that really governs is the paper that has a bullet wrapped up in it. . . . Vote! Bah! When you vote you only change the names of the cabinet. When you shoot, you pull down governments, inaugurate new epochs, abolish old orders and set up new. Is that historically true, Mr. Learned Man, or is it not?

Cusins. It is historically true. I loathe having to admit it. I repudiate your sentiments. I abhor your nature. I defy you in every possible way. Still, it is true. But it ought not to be true. *Undershaft.* Ought, ought, ought, ought, ought! Are you going to spend your life saying ought, like the rest of our moralists? Turn your oughts into shells, man. Come and make explosives with me. The history of the world is the history of those who had the courage to embrace this truth.

"Major Barbara" is one of the most revolutionary plays. In any other but dramatic form the sentiments uttered therein would have condemned the author to long imprisonment for inciting to sedition and violence.

Shaw the Fabian would be the first to repudiate such utterances as rank Anarchy, "impractical, brain cracked and criminal." But Shaw the dramatist is closer to life—closer to reality, closer to the historic truth that the people wrest only as much liberty as they have the intelligence to want and the courage to take.

JOHN GALSWORTHY

The power of the modern drama as an interpreter of the pressing questions of our time is perhaps nowhere evident as clearly as it is in England to-day.

Indeed, while other countries have come almost to a standstill in dramatic art, England is the most productive at the present time. Nor can it be said that quantity has been achieved at the expense of quality, which is only too often the case.

The most prolific English dramatist, John Galsworthy, is at the same time a great artist whose dramatic quality can be compared with that of only one other living writer, namely, Gerhart Hauptmann. Galsworthy, even as Hauptmann, is neither a propagandist nor a moralist. His background is life, "that palpitating life," which is the root of all sorrow and joy.

His attitude toward dramatic art is given in the following words:

"I look upon the stage as the great beacon light of civilization, but the drama should lead the social thought of the time and not direct or dictate it.

"The great duty of the dramatist is to present life as it really is. A true story, if told sincerely, is the strongest moral argument that can be put on the stage. It is the business of the dramatist so to present the characters in his picture of life that the inherent moral is brought to light without any lecturing on his part.

"Moral codes in themselves are, after all, not lasting, but a true picture of life is. A man may preach a strong lesson in a play which may exist for a day, but if he succeeds in presenting real life itself in such a manner as to carry with it a certain moral inspiration, the force of the message need never be lost, for a new interpretation to fit the spirit of the time can renew its vigor and power."

John Galsworthy has undoubtedly succeeded in presenting real life. It is this that makes him so thoroughly human and universal.

STRIFE

Not since Hauptmann's "Weavers" was placed before the thoughtful public, has there appeared anything more stirring than "Strife."

Its theme is a strike in the Trenartha Tin Plate Works, on the borders of England and Wales. The play largely centers about the two dominant figures: *John Anthony,* the President of the Company, rigid, autocratic and uncompromising; he is unwilling to make the slightest concession, although the men have been out for six months and are in a condition of semi-starvation. On the other hand there is *David Roberts,* an uncompromising revolutionist, whose devotion to the workers and the cause of freedom is at red-white heat. Between them are the strikers, worn and weary with the terrible struggle, driven and tortured by the awful sight of poverty at home.

At a directors' meeting, attended by the Company's representatives from London, *Edgar Anthony,* the President's son and a man of kindly feeling, pleads in behalf of the strikers.

Edgar. I don't see how we can get over it that to go on like this means starvation to the men's wives and families . . . It won't kill the shareholders to miss a dividend or two; I don't see that *that's* reason enough for knuckling under.

Wilder. H'm! Shouldn't be a bit surprised if that brute Roberts hadn't got us down here with the very same idea. I hate a man with a grievance.

Edgar. We didn't pay him enough for his discovery. I always said that at the time.

Wilder. We paid him five hundred and a bonus of two hundred three years later. If that's not enough! What does he want, for goodness' sake?

Trench. Company made a hundred thousand out of his brains, and paid him seven hundred—that's the way he goes on, sir.

Wilder. The man's a rank agitator! Look here, I hate the Unions. But now we've got Harness here let's get him to settle the whole thing.

Harness, the trade union official, speaks in favor of compromise. In the beginning of the strike the union had withdrawn its support, because the workers had used their own judgment in deciding to strike.

Harness. I'm quite frank with you. We were forced to withhold our support from your men because some of their demands are in excess of current rates. I expect to make them withdraw those demands to-day. . . . Now, I want to see something fixed upon before I go back tonight. Can't we have done with this old-fashioned tug-of-war business? What good's it doing you? Why don't you recognize once for all that these people are men like yourselves, and want what's good for them just as you want what's good for you. . . . There's just one very simple question I'd like to put to you. Will you pay your men one penny more than they force you to pay them?

Of course not. With trade unionism lacking in true solidarity, and the workers not conscious of their power, why should the Company pay one penny more? *David Roberts* is the only one who fully understands the situation.

Roberts. Justice from London? What are you talking about, Henry Thomas? Have you gone silly? We know very well what we are—discontented dogs—never satisfied. What did the Chairman tell me up in London? That I didn't know what I was talking about. I was a foolish, uneducated man, that knew nothing of the wants of the men I spoke for. . . . I have this to say—and first as to their condition. . . . Ye can't squeeze them any more. Every man of us is well nigh starving. Ye wonder why I tell ye that? Every man of us is going short. We can't be no worse off than we've been these weeks past. Ye needn't think that by waiting ye'll drive us to come in. We'll die first, the whole lot of us. The men have sent for ye to know, once and for all, whether ye are going to grant them their demands. . . . Ye know best whether ye can afford your tyranny—but this I tell ye: If ye think the men will give way the least part of an inch, ye're making the worst mistake ye ever made. Ye think because the Union is not supporting us—more shame to it!—that we'll be coming on our knees to you one fine morning. Ye think because the men have got their wives an' families to think of—that it's just a question of a week or two— . . .

The appalling state of the strikers is demonstrated by the women: *Anna Roberts,* sick with heart trouble and slowly dying for want of warmth and nourishment; *Mrs. Rous,* so accustomed to privation that her present poverty seems easy compared with the misery of her whole life.

Into this dismal environment comes *Enid,* the President's daughter, with delicacies and jams for *Annie.* Like many women of her station she imagines that a little sympathy will bridge the chasm between the classes, or as her father says, "You think with your gloved hands you can cure the troubles of the century."

Enid does not know the life of *Annie Roberts'* class: that it is all a gamble from the "time 'e 's born to the time 'e dies."

Mrs. Roberts. Roberts says workin' folk have always lived from hand to mouth. Sixpence to-day is worth more than a shillin' to-morrow, that's what they say. . . . He says that when a working man's baby is born, it's a toss-up from breath to breath whether it ever draws another, and so on all 'is life; an' when he comes to be old, it's the workhouse or the grave. He says that without a man is very near, and pinches and stints 'imself and 'is children to save, there can be neither surplus nor security. That's why he wouldn't have no children, not though I wanted them.

The strikers' meeting is a masterly study of mass psychology,—the men swayed hither and thither by the different speakers and not knowing whither to go. It is the smooth-tongued *Harness* who first weakens their determination to hold out.

Harness. Cut your demands to the right pattern, and we'll see you through; refuse, and don't expect me to waste my time coming down here again. I'm not the sort that speaks at random, as you ought to know by this time. If you're the sound men I take you for—no matter who advises you against it—you'll make up your minds to come in, and trust to us to get your terms. Which is it to be? Hands together, and victory—or—the starvation you've got now?

Then *Old Thomas* appeals to their religious sentiments:

Thomas. It iss not London; it iss not the Union—it iss Nature. It iss no disgrace whateffer to a potty to give in to Nature. For this Nature iss a fery pig thing; it is pigger than what a man is. There is more years to my hett than to the hett of anyone here. It is a man's pisness to pe pure, honest, just, and merciful. That's what Chapel tells you. . . . We're going the roat to tamnation. An' so I say to all of you. If ye co against Chapel I will not pe with you, nor will any other Got-fearing man.

At last *Roberts* makes his plea, *Roberts* who has given his all—brain, heart and blood—aye, sacrificed even his wife to the cause. By sheer force of eloquence and sincerity he stays his fickle comrades long enough at least to listen to him, though they are too broken to rise to his great dignity and courage.

Roberts. You don't want to hear me then? You'll listen to Rous and to that old man, but not to me. You'll listen to Sim Harness of the Union that's treated you so *fair;* maybe you'll listen to those men from London . . . You love their feet on your necks, don't you? . . . Am I a liar, a coward, a traitor? If only I were, ye'd listen to me, I'm sure. Is there a man of you here who has less to gain by striking? Is there a man of you that had more to lose? Is there a man among you who has given up eight hundred pounds since this trouble began? Come, now, is there? How much has Thomas given up—ten pounds or five or what? You listened to him, and what had he to say? "None can pretend," he said, "that I'm not a believer in principle—but when Nature says: 'No further,' 'tes going against Nature!" I tell you if a man cannot say to Nature: "Budge me from this if ye can!"—his principles are but his belly. "Oh, but," Thomas says, "a man can be pure and honest, just and merciful, and take off his hat to Nature." I tell you Nature's neither pure nor honest, just not merciful. You chaps that live over the hill, an' go home dead beat in the dark on a snowy night—don't ye fight your way every inch of it? Do ye go lyin' down an' trustin' to the tender mercies of this merciful Nature? Try it and you'll soon know with what ye've got to deal. 'Tes only by that *(he strikes a blow with his clenched fist)* in Nature's face that a man can be a man. "Give in," says Thomas; "go down on your knees; throw up your foolish fight, an' perhaps," he said, "perhaps your enemy will chuck you down a crust." . . . And what did he say about Chapel? "Chapel's against it," he said. "She's against it." Well, if Chapel and Nature go hand in hand, it's the first I've ever heard of it. Surrendering's the work of cowards and traitors. . . . You've felt the pinch o't in your bellies. You've forgotten what that fight 'as been; many times I have told you; I will tell you now this once again. The fight o' the country's body and blood against a blood-sucker. The fight of those that spend themselves with every blow they strike and every breath they draw, against a thing that fattens on them, and grows and grows by the law of *merciful* Nature. That thing is Capital! A thing that buys the sweat o' men's brows, and the tortures o' their brains, at its own price. Don't I know that? Wasn't the work o' my brains bought for seven hundred pounds, and hasn't one hundred thousand pounds been gained them by that seven hundred without the stirring of a finger. It is a thing that will take as much and give you as little as it can. That's Capital! A thing that will say—"I'm very sorry for you, poor fellows—you have a cruel time of it, I know," but will not give one sixpence of its dividends to help you have a better time. That's Capital! Tell me, for all their talk, is there one of them that will consent to another penny on the Income Tax to help the poor? That's Capital! A white-faced, stony-hearted monster! Ye have got it on its knees; are ye to give up at the last minute to save your miserable bodies pain? When I went this morning to those old men from London, I looked into their very 'earts. One of them was sitting there—Mr. Scantlebury, a mass of flesh nourished on us: sittin' there for all the world like the shareholders in this Company, that sit not moving tongue nor finger, takin' dividends—a great dumb ox that can only be roused when its food is threatened. I looked into his eyes and I saw *he was afraid*—afraid for himself and his dividends, afraid for his fees, afraid of the very shareholders he stands for; and all but one of them's afraid—like children that get into a wood at night, and start at every rustle of the leaves. I ask you, men—give me a free hand to tell them: "Go you back to London. The men have nothing for you!" Give me that, and I swear to you, within a week you shall have from London all you want. 'Tis not for this little moment of time we're fighting, not for *ourselves,* our own little bodies, and their wants, 'tis for all those that come after throughout all time. Oh! men—for the love o' them, don't roll up another stone upon their heads, don't help to blacken the sky, an' let the bitter sea in over them. They're welcome to the worst that can happen to me, to the worst that can happen to us all, aren't they—aren't they? If we can shake the white-faced monster with the bloody lips, that has sucked the life out of ourselves, our wives, and children, since the world began. If we have not the hearts of men to stand against it breast to breast, and eye to eye, and force it backward till it cry for mercy, it will go on sucking life; and we shall stay forever what we are, less than the very dogs.

Consistency is the greatest crime of our commercial age. No matter how intense the spirit or how important the man, the moment he will not allow himself to be used or sell his principles, he is thrown on the dust heap. Such is the fate of *Anthony,* The President of the Company, and of *David Roberts.* To be sure they represent opposite poles—poles antagonistic to each other, poles divided by a terrible gap that can never be bridged over. Yet they share a common fate. *Anthony* is the embodiment of conservatism, of old ideas, of iron methods:

Anthony. I have been Chairman of this Company since its inception two and thirty years ago ... I have had to do with "men" for fifty years; I've always stood up to them; I have never been beaten yet. I have fought the men of this Company four times, and four times I have beaten them. . . . The men have been treated justly, they have had fair wages, we have always been ready to listen to complaints. It has been said that times have changed; if they have, I have not changed with them. Neither will I. It has been said that masters and men are equal! Cant! There can only be one master in a house! Where two men meet the better man will rule. It has been said that Capital and Labor have the same interests. Cant! Their interests are as wide asunder as the poles. It has been said that the Board is only part of a machine. Cant! We *are* the machine; its brains and sinews; it is for us to lead and to determine what is to be done; and to do it without fear or favor. Fear of the men! Fear of the shareholders! Fear of our own shadows! Before I am like that, I hope to die. There is only one way of treating "men"—with the iron hand. This half-and-half business, the half-and-half manners of this generation, has brought all this upon us. Sentiments and softness and what this young man, no doubt, would call his social policy. You can't eat cake and have it! This middle-class sentiment, or socialism, or whatever it may be, is rotten. Masters are masters, men are men! Yield one demand, and they will make it six. They are like Oliver Twist, asking for more. If I were in *their* place I should be the same. But I am not in their place. . . . I have been accused of being a domineering tyrant, thinking only of my pride—I am thinking of the future of this country, threatened with the black waters of confusion, threatened with mob government, threatened with what I cannot say. If by any conduct of mine I help to bring this on us, I shall be ashamed to look my fellows in the face. Before I put this amendment to the Board, I have one more word to say. If it is carried, it means that we shall fail in the duty that we owe to all Capital. It means that we shall fail in the duty that we owe ourselves.

We may not like this adherence to old, reactionary notions, and yet there is something admirable in the courage and consistency of this man; nor is he half as dangerous to the interests of the oppressed as our sentimental and soft reformers who rob with nine fingers, and give libraries with the tenth; who grind human beings and spend millions of dollars in social research work. *Anthony* is a worthy foe; to fight such a foe, one must learn to meet him in open battle.

David Roberts has all the mental and moral attributes of his adversary, coupled with the spirit of revolt and the inspiration of modern ideas. He, too, is consistent: he wants nothing for his class short of complete victory.

It is inevitable that compromise and petty interest should triumph until the masses become imbued with the spirit of a *David Roberts*. Will they ever? Prophecy is not the vocation of the dramatist, yet the moral lesson is evident. One cannot help realizing that the workingmen will have to use methods hitherto unfamiliar to them; that they will have to discard the elements in their midst that are forever seeking to reconcile the irreconcilable—Capital and Labor. They will have to learn that men like *David Roberts* are the very forces that have revolutionized the world and thus paved the way for emancipation out of the clutches of the "white-faced monster with bloody lips," toward a brighter horizon, a freer life, and a truer recognition of human values.

JUSTICE

No subject of equal social import has received such thoughtful consideration in recent years as the question of Crime and Punishment. A number of
books by able writers, both in Europe and this country—preëminently among
them "Prison Memoirs of an Anarchist," by Alexander Berkman—discuss
this topic from the historic, psychologic, and social standpoint, the consensus
of opinion being that present penal institutions and our methods of coping
with crime have in every respect proved inadequate as well as wasteful. This
new attitude toward one of the gravest social wrongs has now also found
dramatic interpretation in Galsworthy's "Justice."

The play opens in the office of *James How & Sons*, solicitors. The senior
clerk, *Robert Cokeson*, discovers that a check he had issued for nine pounds
has been forged to ninety. By elimination, suspicion falls upon *William
Falder*, the junior office clerk. The latter is in love with a married woman,
the abused and ill-treated wife of a brutal drunkard. Pressed by his employer, a severe yet not unkindly man, *Falder* confesses the forgery, pleading the
dire necessity of his sweetheart, *Ruth Honeywill*, with whom he had planned
to escape to save her from the unbearable brutality of her husband.

Falder. Oh! sir, look over it! I'll pay the money back—I will, I promise.

Notwithstanding the entreaties of young *Walter How*, who holds modern
ideas, his father, a moral and law-respecting citizen, turns *Falder* over to the
police.

The second act, in the court room, shows Justice in the very process of
manufacture. The scene equals in dramatic power and psychologic verity the
great court scene in "Resurrection." Young *Falder*, a nervous and rather
weakly youth of twenty-three, stands before the bar. *Ruth*, his faithful
sweetheart, full of love and devotion, burns with anxiety to save the young
man, whose affection for her has brought about his present predicament.
Falder is defended by *Lawyer Frome*, whose speech to the jury is a master-
piece of social philosophy. He does not attempt to dispute the mere fact that
his client had altered the check; and though he pleads temporary aberration in
his defense, the argument is based on a social consciousness as fundamental
and all-embracing as the roots of our social ills—"the background of life, that

palpitating life which always lies behind the commission of a crime." He shows *Falder* to have faced the alternative of seeing the beloved woman murdered by her brutal husband, whom she cannot divorce, or of taking the law into his own hands. He pleads with the jury not to turn the weak young man into a criminal by condemning him to prison.

Frome. Men like the prisoner are destroyed daily under our law for want of that human insight which sees them as they are, patients, and not criminals. . . . Justice is a machine that, when someone has given it a starting push, rolls on of itself. . . . Is this young man to be ground to pieces under this machine for an act which, at the worst, was one of weakness? Is he to become a member of the luckless crews that man those dark, ill-starred ships called prisons? . . . I urge you, gentlemen, do not ruin this young man. For as a result of those four minutes, ruin, utter and irretrievable, stares him in the face. . . . The rolling of the chariot wheels of Justice over this boy began when it was decided to prosecute him.

But the chariot of Justice rolls mercilessly on, for—as the learned Judge says—

"Your counsel has made an attempt to trace your offense back to what he seems to suggest is a defect in the marriage law; he has made an attempt also to show that to punish you with further imprisonment would be unjust. I do not follow him in these flights. *The Law is what it is*—a majestic edifice, sheltering all of us, each stone of which rests on another. I am concerned only with its administration. The crime you have committed is a very serious one. I cannot feel it in accordance with my duty to Society to exercise the powers I have in your favor. You will go to penal servitude for three years."

In prison the young, inexperienced convict soon finds himself the victim of the terrible "system." The authorities admit that young *Falder* is mentally and physically "in bad shape," but nothing can be done in the matter: many others are in a similar position, and "the quarters are inadequate."

The third scene of the third act is heart-gripping in its silent force. The whole scene is a pantomime, taking place in *Falder's* prison cell.

"In fast-falling daylight, *Falder*, in his stockings, is seen standing motionless, with his head inclined towards the door, listening. He moves a little closer to the door, his stockinged feet making no noise. He stops at the door. He is trying harder and harder to hear something, any little thing that is going on outside. He springs suddenly upright—as if at a sound—and remains perfectly motionless. Then, with a heavy sigh, he moves to his work, and stands looking at it, with his head down; he does a stitch or two, having the air of a man so lost in sadness that each stitch is, as it were, a coming to life. Then, turning abruptly, he begins pacing his cell, moving his head, like an animal pacing its cage. He stops again at the door, listens, and, placing the palms of his hands against it, with his fingers spread out, leans his forehead against the iron. Turning from it, presently, he moves slowly back towards the window, tracing his way with his finger along the top line of the distemper that runs round the wall. He stops under the window, and, picking up the lid of one of the tins, peers into it. It has grown very nearly dark. Suddenly the lid falls out of his hand with a clatter—the only sound that has broken the silence—and he stands staring intently at the wall where the stuff of the shirt is hanging rather white in the darkness—he seems to be seeing somebody or something there. There is a sharp tap and click; the cell light behind the glass screen has been turned up. The cell is brightly lighted. *Falder* is seen gasping for breath.

"A sound from far away, as of distant, dull beating on thick metal, is suddenly audible. *Falder* shrinks back, not able to bear this sudden clamor. But the sound grows, as though some great tumbril were rolling towards the cell. And gradually it seems to hypnotize him. He begins creeping inch by inch nearer to the door. The banging sound, traveling from cell to cell, draws closer and closer; *Falder's* hands are seen moving as if his spirit had already joined in this beating; and the sound swells until it seems to have entered the very cell. He suddenly raises his clenched fists.

"Panting violently, he flings himself at his door, and beats on it."

Falder leaves the prison, a broken ticket-of-leave man, the stamp of the convict upon his brow, the iron of misery in his soul.

Falder. I seem to be struggling against a thing that's all round me. I can't explain it: it's as if I was in a net; as fast as I cut it here, it grows up there. I didn't act as I ought to have, about references; but what are you to do? You must have them. And that made me afraid, and I left. In fact, I'm—I'm afraid all the time now.

Thanks to *Ruth's* pleading, the firm of *James How & Son* is willing to take *Falder* back in their employ, on condition that he give up *Ruth*. *Falder* resents this:

Falder. I couldn't give her up. I couldn't! Oh, sir! I'm all she's got to look to. And I'm sure she's all I've got.

It is then that *Falder* learns the awful news that the woman he loves had been driven by the chariot wheel of Justice to sell herself.

Ruth. I tried making skirts . . . cheap things. It was the best I could get, but I never made more than ten shillings a week, buying my own cotton and working all day; I hardly ever got to bed till past twelve. I kept at it for nine months. . . . It was starvation for the children. . . . And then . . . my employer happened—he's happened ever since.

At this terrible psychologic moment the police appear to drag *Falder* back to prison for failing to report to the authorities as ticket-of-leave man.

Completely overcome by the inexorability of his fate, *Falder* throws himself down the stairs, breaking his neck.

The socio-revolutionary significance of "Justice" consists not only in the portrayal of the inhuman system which grinds the Falders and Honeywills, but even more so in the utter helplessness of society as expressed in the words of the Senior Clerk, *Cokeson,* "No one'll touch him now! Never again! He's safe with gentle Jesus!"

THE PIGEON

John Galsworthy calls this play a fantasy. To me it seems cruelly real: it demonstrates that the best human material is crushed in the fatal mechanism of our life. "The Pigeon" also discloses to us the inadequacy of charity, individual and organized, to cope with poverty, as well as the absurdity of reformers and experimenters who attempt to patch up effects while they ignore the causes.

Christopher Wellwyn, an artist, a man deeply in sympathy with all human sorrow and failings, generously shares his meager means with everyone who applies to him for help.

His daughter *Ann* is of a more practical turn of mind. She cannot understand that giving is as natural and necessary to her father as light and air; indeed, the greatest joy in life.

Perhaps *Ann* is actuated by anxiety for her father who is so utterly "hopeless" that he would give away his "last pair of trousers." From her point of view "people who beg are rotters": decent folk would not stoop to begging. But *Christopher Wellwyn's* heart is too full of humanity to admit of such a straight-laced attitude. "We're not all the same. . . . One likes to be friendly. What's the use of being alive if one isn't?" Unfortunately most people are not alive to the tragedies around them. They are often unthinking mechanisms, mere tabulating machines, like *Alfred Calway,* the Professor, who believes that "we're to give the State all we can spare, to make the undeserving deserving." Or as *Sir Hoxton,* the Justice of the Peace, who insists that "we ought to support private organizations for helping the deserving, and damn the undeserving." Finally there is the *Canon* who religiously seeks the middle road and "wants a little of both."

When *Ann* concludes that her father is the despair of all social reformers, she is but expressing a great truism; namely, that social reform is a cold and bloodless thing that can find no place in the glowing humanity of *Christopher Wellwyn.*

It is Christmas Eve, the birth of Him who came to proclaim "Peace on earth, good will to all." *Christopher Wellwyn* is about to retire when he is disturbed by a knock on the door.

The snow-covered, frost-pinched figure of *Guinevere Megan* appears. She is a flower-seller to whom *Wellwyn* had once given his card that she might find him in case of need. She comes to him when the rest of the world has passed her by, forlorn and almost as dead as her violets which no one cares to buy.

At sight of her misery *Wellwyn* forgets his daughter's practical admonition and his promise to her not to be "a fool." He treats the flower-seller tenderly, makes her warm and comfortable. He has barely time to show *Guinevere* into his model's room, when another knock is heard. This time it is *Ferrand,* "an alien," a globe trotter without means,—a tramp whom *Wellwyn* had once met in the Champs-Elysées. Without food for days and unable to endure the cold, *Ferrand* too comes to the artist.

Ferrand. If I had not found you, Monsieur—I would have been a little hole in the river to-night—I was so discouraged. . . . And to think that in a few minutes He will be born! . . . The world would reproach you for your goodness to me. Monsieur, if He himself were on earth now, there would be a little heap of gentlemen writing to the journals every day to call him sloppee sentimentalist! And what is veree funny, these gentlemen they would all be most strong Christians. But that will not trouble you, Monsieur; I saw well from the first that you are no Christian. You have so kind a face.

Ferrand has deeper insight into the character of *Christopher Wellwyn* than his daughter. He knows that the artist would not judge nor could he refuse one whom misery stares in the face. Even the third visitor of *Wellwyn,* the old cabman *Timson,* with more whisky than bread in his stomach, receives the same generous reception as the other two.

The next day *Ann* calls a council of war. The learned Professor, *Alfred Calway;* the wise judge, *Sir Thomas Hoxton;* and the professional Christian, *Edward Bertley*—the Canon—are summoned to decide the fate of the three outcasts.

There are few scenes in dramatic literature so rich in satire, so deep in the power of analysis as the one in which these eminent gentlemen discuss human destiny. *Canon Bertley* is emphatic that it is necessary to "remove the temptation and reform the husband of the flower-seller."

Bertley. Now, what is to be done?

Mrs. Megan. I could get an unfurnished room, if I'd the money to furnish it.

Bertley. Never mind the money. What I want to find in you is repentance.

Those who are engaged in saving souls cannot be interested in such trifles as money matters, nor to understand the simple truth that if the Megans did not have to bother with making a "livin'," repentance would take care of itself.

The other two gentlemen are more worldly, since law and science cannot experiment with such elusive things as the soul. *Professor Calway* opines that *Timson* is a congenital case, to be put under observation, while *Judge Hoxton* decides that he must be sent to prison.

Calway. Is it, do you think, chronic unemployment with a vagrant tendency? Or would it be nearer the mark to say: Vagrancy— Dipsomaniac? ... By the look of his face, as far as one can see it, I should say there was a leaning towards mania. I know the treatment.

Hoxton. Hundreds of these fellows before me in my time. The only thing is a sharp lesson!

Calway. I disagree. I've seen the man; what he requires is steady control, and the Dobbins treatment.

Hoxton. Not a bit of it! He wants one for his knob! Bracing him up! It's the only thing!

Calway. You're moving backwards, Sir Thomas. I've told you before, convinced reactionaryism, in these days—The merest sense of continuity—a simple instinct for order—

Hoxton. The only way to get order, sir, is to bring the disorderly up with a round turn. You people without practical experience—

Calway. The question is a much wider one, Sir Thomas.

Hoxton. No, sir, I repeat if the country once commits itself to your views of reform, it's as good as doomed.

Calway. I seem to have heard that before, Sir Thomas. And let me say at once that your hitty-missy cart-load of bricks régime—

Hoxton. Is a deuced sight better, sir, than your grandmotherly methods. What the old fellow wants is a shock! With all this socialistic molly-coddling, you're losing sight of the individual.

Calway. You, sir, with your "devil take the hindmost," have never seen him.

The farce ends by each one insisting on the superiority of his own pet theory, while misery continues to stalk white-faced through the streets.

Three months later *Ann* determines to rescue her father from his disreputable proclivities by removing with him to a part of the city where their address will remain unknown to his beggar friends and acquaintances.

While their belongings are being removed, *Canon Bertley* relates the trouble he had with *Mrs. Megan.*

Bertley. I consulted with Calway and he advised me to try a certain institution. We got her safely in—excellent place; but, d'you know, she broke out three weeks ago. And since—I've heard—hopeless, I'm afraid—quite! . . . I'm sometimes tempted to believe there's nothing for some of these poor folk but to pray for death.

Wellwyn. The Professor said he felt there was nothing for some of these poor devils but a lethal chamber.

What is science for if not to advise a lethal chamber? It's the easiest way to dispose of "the unfit" and to supply learned professors with the means of comfortable livelihood.

Yet there is *Ferrand,* the vagabond, the social outcast who has never seen the inside of a university, propounding a philosophy which very few professors even dream of:

Ferrand. While I was on the road this time I fell ill of a fever. It seemed to me in my illness that I saw the truth—how I was wasting in this world—I would never be good for anyone—nor anyone for me—all would go by, and I never of it—fame, and fortune, and peace, even the necessities of life, ever mocking me. And I saw, so plain, that I should be vagabond all my days, and my days short; I dying in the end the death of a dog. I saw it all in my fever—clear as that flame—there was nothing for us others, but the herb of death. And so I wished to die. I told no one of my fever. I lay out on the ground—it was verree cold. But they would not let me die on the roads of their parishes— They took me to an Institution. I looked in their eyes while I lay there, and I saw more clear than the blue heaven that they thought it best that I should die, although they would not let me. Then naturally my spirit rose, and I said: "So much the worse for you. I will live a little more." One is made like that! Life is sweet. That little girl you had there, Monsieur—in her too there is something of wild savage. She must have joy of life. I have seen her since I came back. She has embraced the life of joy. It is not quite the same thing. She is lost, Monsieur, as a stone that sinks in water. I can see, if she cannot. . . . For the great part of mankind, to see anything—is fatal. No, Monsieur. To be so near to death has done me good; I shall not lack courage any more till the wind blows on my grave. Since I saw you, Monsieur, I have been in three Institutions. They are palaces. . . . One little thing they lack—those palaces. It is understanding of the 'uman heart. In them tame birds pluck wild birds naked. Ah! Monsieur, I am loafer, waster—what you like—for all that, poverty is my only crime. If I were rich, should I not be simply verree original, 'ighly respected, with soul above commerce, traveling to see the world? And that young girl, would she not be "that charming ladee," "veree chic, you know!" And the old Tims—good old-fashioned gentleman—drinking his liquor well. Eh! bien—what are we now? Dark beasts, despised by all. That is life, Monsieur. Monsieur, it is just that. You understand. When we are with you we feel something—here— If I had one prayer to make, it would be, "Good God, give me to understand!" Those sirs, with their theories, they can clean our skins and chain our 'abits—that soothes for them the aesthetic sense; it gives them too their good little importance. But our spirits they cannot touch, for they nevare understand. Without that, Monsieur, all is dry as a parched skin of orange. Monsieur, of their industry I say nothing. They do a good work while they attend with their theories to the sick and the tame old, and the good unfortunate deserving. Above all to the little children. But, Monsieur, when all is done, there are always us hopeless ones. What can they do with me, Monsieur, with that girl, or with that old man? Ah! Monsieur, we too, 'ave our qualities, we others—it wants you courage to undertake a career like mine, or like that young girl's. We wild ones—we know a thousand times more of life than ever will those sirs. They waste their time trying to make rooks white. Be kind to us if you will, or let us alone like Mees Ann, but do not try to change our skins. Leave us to live, or leave us to die when we like in the free air. If you do not wish of us, you have but to shut your pockets and your doors—we shall die the faster. . . . If you cannot, how is it our fault? The harm we do to others—is it so much? If I am criminal, dangerous—shut me up! I would not pity myself—nevare. But we in whom something moves—like that flame, Monsieur, that cannot keep still—we others— we are not many—that must have motion in our lives, do not let them make us prisoners, with their theories, because we are not like them—it is life itself they would enclose! . . . The good God made me so that I would rather walk a whole month of nights, hungry, with the stars, than sit one single day making round business on an office stool! It is not to my advantage. I cannot help it that I am a vagabond. What would you have? It is stronger than me. Monsieur, I say to you things I have never said. Monsieur! Are you really English? The English are so civilized.

Truly the English are highly "civilized"; else it would be impossible to explain why of all the nations on earth, the Anglo-Saxons should be the only ones to punish attempts at suicide.

Society makes no provision whatever for the Timsons, the Ferrands and Mrs. Megans. It has closed the door in their face, denying them a seat at the table of life. Yet when *Guinevere Megan* attempts to drown herself, a benevolent constable drags her out and a Christian Judge sends her to the workhouse.

Constable. Well, sir, we can't get over the facts, can we? . . . You know what soocide amounts to—it's an awkward job.

Wellwyn. But look here, Constable, as a reasonable man— This poor wretched little girl—*you* know what that life means better than anyone! Why! It's to her credit to try and jump out of it!

Constable. Can't neglect me duty, sir; that's impossible.

Wellwyn. Of all the d—d topsy-turvy—! Not a soul in the world wants her alive—and now she is to be prosecuted for trying to go where everyone wishes her.

Is it necessary to dwell on the revolutionary significance of this cruel reality? It is so all-embracing in its sweep, so penetrating of the topsy-turviness of our civilization, with all its cant and artifice, so powerful in its condemnation of our cheap theories and cold institutionalism which freezes the soul and destroys the best and finest in our being. The Wellwyns, Ferrands, and Megans are the stuff out of which a real humanity might be fashioned. They feel the needs of their fellows, and whatever is in their power to give, they give as nature does, unreservedly. But the Hoxtons, Calways and Bertleys have turned the world into a dismal prison and mankind into monotonous, gray, dull shadows.

The professors, judges, and preachers cannot meet the situation. Neither can *Wellwyn,* to be sure. And yet his very understanding of the differentiation of human nature, and his sympathy with the inevitable reaction of conditions upon it, bring the Wellwyns much closer to the solution of our evils than all the Hoxtons, Calways and Bertleys put together. This deep conception of social factors is in itself perhaps the most significant lesson taught in "The Pigeon."

STANLEY HOUGHTON

HINDLE WAKES

In Stanley Houghton, who died last year, the drama lost a talented and brave artist. Brave, because he had the courage to touch one of the most sensitive spots of Puritanism—woman's virtue. Whatever else one may criticise or attack, the sacredness of virtue must remain untouched. It is the last fetish which even so-called liberal-minded people refuse to destroy.

To be sure, the attitude towards this holy of holies has of late years undergone a considerable change. It is beginning to be felt in ever-growing circles that love is its own justification, requiring no sanction of either religion or law. The revolutionary idea, however, that woman may, even as man, follow the urge of her nature, has never before been so sincerely and radically expressed.

The message of "Hindle Wakes" is therefore of inestimable value, inasmuch as it dispels the fog of the silly sentimentalism and disgusting bombast that declares woman a thing apart from nature—one who neither does nor must crave the joys of life permissible to man.

Hindle is a small weaving town, symbolically representing the wakefulness of every small community to the shortcomings of its neighbors.

Christopher Hawthorne and *Nathaniel Jeffcote* had begun life together as lads in the cotton mill. But while *Christopher* was always a timid and shrinking boy, *Nathaniel* was aggressive and ambitious. When the play opens, *Christopher,* though an old man, is still a poor weaver; *Nathaniel,* on the contrary, has reached the top of financial and social success. He is the owner of the biggest mill; is wealthy, influential, and withal a man of power. For *Nathaniel Jeffcote* always loved power and social approval. Speaking of the motor he bought for his only son *Alan,* he tells his wife:

Jeffcote. Why did I buy a motor-car? Not because I wanted to go motoring. I hate it. I bought it so that people could see Alan driving about in it, and say, "There's Jeffcote's lad in his new car. It cost five hundred quid."

However, *Nathaniel* is a "square man," and when facing an emergency, not chary with justice and always quick to decide in its favor.

125

The *Jeffcotes* center all their hopes on *Alan*, their only child, who is to inherit their fortune and business. *Alan* is engaged to *Beatrice*, the lovely, sweet daughter of *Sir Timothy Farrar*, and all is joyous at the Jeffcotes'.

Down in the valley of Hindle live the *Hawthornes*, humble and content, as behooves God-fearing workers. They too have ambitions in behalf of their daughter *Fanny*, strong, willful and self-reliant,—qualities molded in the hard grind of *Jeffcote's* mill, where she had begun work as a tot.

During the "bank holiday" *Fanny* with her chum *Mary* goes to a neighboring town for an outing. There they meet two young men, *Alan Jeffcote* and his friend. *Fanny* departs with *Alan*, and they spend a glorious time together. On the way home *Mary* is drowned. As a result of the accident the *Hawthornes* learn that their daughter had not spent her vacation with *Mary*. When *Fanny* returns, they question her, and though she at first refuses to give an account of herself, they soon discover that the girl had passed the time with a man,—young *Alan Jeffcote*. Her parents are naturally horrified, and decide to force the *Jeffcotes* to have *Alan* marry *Fanny*.

In the old mother of *Fanny* the author has succeeded in giving a most splendid characterization of the born drudge, hardened by her long struggle with poverty, and grown shrewd in the ways of the world. She knows her daughter so little, however, that she believes *Fanny* had schemed the affair with *Alan* in the hope that she might force him to marry her. In her imagination the old woman already sees *Fanny* as the mistress of the Jeffcote estate. She persuades her husband to go immediately to the *Jeffcotes*, and though it is very late at night, the old man is forced to start out on his disagreeable errand.

Jeffcote, a man of integrity, is much shocked at the news brought to him by old *Hawthorne*. Nevertheless he will not countenance the wrong.

Jeffcote. I'll see you're treated right. Do you hear?
Christopher. I can't ask for more than that.
Jeffcote. I'll see you're treated right.

Young *Alan* had never known responsibility. Why should he, with so much wealth awaiting him? When confronted by his father and told that he must marry *Fanny*, he fights hard against it. It may be said, in justice to *Alan*, that he really loves his betrothed, *Beatrice*, though such a circumstance has never deterred the Alans from having a lark with another girl.

The young man resents his father's command to marry the mill girl. But when even *Beatrice* insists that he belongs to *Fanny, Alan* unwillingly consents. *Beatrice,* a devout Christian, believes in renunciation.

Beatrice. I do need you, Alan. So much that nothing on earth could make me break off our engagement, if I felt that it was at all possible to let it go on. But it isn't. It's impossible.

Alan. And you want me to marry Fanny?

Beatrice. Yes. Oh, Alan! can't you see what a splendid sacrifice you have it in your power to make? Not only to do the right thing, but to give up so much in order to do it.

The *Jeffcotes* and the *Hawthornes* gather to arrange the marriage of their children. It does not occur to them to consult *Fanny* in the matter. Much to their consternation, *Fanny* refuses to abide by the decision of the family council.

Fanny. It's very good of you. You'll hire the parson and get the license and make all the arrangements on your own without consulting me, and I shall have nothing to do save turn up meek as a lamb at the church or registry office or whatever it is. . . . That's just where you make the mistake. I don't want to marry Alan. . . . I mean what I say, and I'll trouble you to talk to me without swearing at me. I'm not one of the family yet.

The dismayed parents, and even *Alan,* plead with her and threaten. But *Fanny* is obdurate. At last *Alan* asks to be left alone with her, confident that he can persuade the girl.

Alan. Look here, Fanny, what's all this nonsense about? . . . Why won't you marry me?

Fanny. You can't understand a girl not jumping at you when she gets the chance, can you? . . . How is it that you aren't going to marry Beatrice Farrar? Weren't you fond of her?

Alan. Very. . . . I gave her up because my father made me.

Fanny. Made you? Good Lord, a chap of your age!

Alan. My father's a man who will have his own way. . . . He can keep me short of brass.

Fanny. Earn some brass.

Alan. I can earn some brass, but it will mean hard work and it'll take time. And, after all, I shan't earn anything like what I get now.

Fanny. Then all you want to wed me for is what you'll get with me? I'm to be given away with a pound of tea, as it were?

Alan. I know why you won't marry me. . . . You're doing it for my sake.

Fanny. Don't you kid yourself, my lad! It isn't because I'm afraid of spoiling your life that I'm refusing you, but because I'm afraid of spoiling mine! That didn't occur to you?

Alan. Look here, Fanny, I promise you I'll treat you fair all the time. You don't need to fear that folk'll look down on you. We shall have too much money for that.

Fanny. I can manage all right on twenty-five bob a week.

Alan. I'm going to fall between two stools. It's all up with *Beatrice,* of course. And if you won't have me I shall have parted from her to no purpose; besides getting kicked out of the house by my father, more than likely! You said you were fond of me once, but it hasn't taken you long to alter.

Fanny. All women aren't built alike. Beatrice is religious. She'll be sorry for you. I was fond of you in a way.

Alan. But you didn't ever really love me?

Fanny. Love you? Good heavens, of course not! Why on earth should I love you? You were just someone to have a bit of fun with. You were an amusement—a lark. How much more did you care for me?

Alan. But it's not the same. I'm a man.

Fanny. You're a man, and I was your little fancy. Well, I'm a woman, and you were my little fancy. You wouldn't prevent a woman enjoying herself as well as a man, if she takes it into her head?

Alan. But do you mean to say that you didn't care any more for me than a fellow cares for any girl he happens to pick up?

Fanny. Yes. Are you shocked?

Alan. It's a bit thick; it is really!

Fanny. You're a beauty to talk!

Alan. It sounds so jolly immoral. I never thought of a girl looking on a chap just like that! I made sure you wanted to marry me if you got the chance.

Fanny. No fear! You're not good enough for me. The chap Fanny Hawthorne weds has got to be made of different stuff from you, my lad. *My* husband, if ever I have one, will be a man, not a fellow who'll throw over his girl at his father's bidding! Strikes me the sons of these rich manufacturers are all much alike. They seem a bit weak in the upper story. It's their father's brass that's too much for them, happen! . . . You've no call to be afraid. I'm not going to disgrace you.

But so long as I've to live my own life I don't see why I shouldn't choose what it's to be.

Unheard of, is it not, that a Fanny should refuse to be made a "good woman," and that she should dare demand the right to live in her own way? It has always been considered the most wonderful event in the life of a girl if a young man of wealth, of position, of station came into her life and said, "I will take you as my wife until death do us part."

But a new type of girlhood is in the making. We are developing the Fannies who learn in the school of life, the hardest, the cruelest and at the same time the most vital and instructive school. Why should *Fanny* marry a young man in order to become "good," any more than that he should marry her in order to become good? Is it not because we have gone on for centuries believing that woman's value, her integrity and position in society center about her sex and consist only in her virtue, and that all other usefulness weighs naught in the balance against her "purity"? If she dare express her sex as the Fannies do, we deny her individual and social worth, and stamp her fallen.

The past of a man is never questioned: no one inquires how many Fannies have been in his life. Yet man has the impudence to expect the Fannies to abstain till he is ready to bestow on them his name.

"Hindle Wakes" is a much needed and important social lesson,—not because it necessarily involves the idea that every girl must have sex experience before she meets the man she loves, but rather that she has the right to satisfy, if she so chooses, her emotional and sex demands like any other need of her mind and body. When the Fannies become conscious of that right, the relation of the sexes will lose the shallow romanticism and artificial exaggeration that mystery has surrounded it with, and assume a wholesome, natural, and therefore healthy and normal expression.

GITHA SOWERBY

RUTHERFORD AND SON

The women's rights women who claim for their sex the most wonderful things in the way of creative achievement, will find it difficult to explain the fact that until the author of "Rutherford and Son" made her appearance, no country had produced a single woman dramatist of note.

That is the more remarkable because woman has since time immemorial been a leading figure in histrionic art. Rachel, Sarah Bernhardt, Eleanore Duse, and scores of others have had few male peers.

It can hardly be that woman is merely a reproducer and not a creator. We have but to recall such creative artists as Charlotte and Emily Brontë, George Sand, George Eliot, Mary Wollstonecraft, Marie Bashkirtshev, Rosa Bonheur, Sophia Kovalevskaya and a host of others, to appreciate that woman has been a creative factor in literature, art and science. Not so in the drama, so far the stronghold exclusively of men.

It is therefore an event for a woman to come to the fore who possesses such dramatic power, realistic grasp and artistic penetration as evidenced by Githa Sowerby.

The circumstance is the more remarkable because Githa Sowerby is, according to her publishers, barely out of her teens; and though she be a genius, her exceptional maturity is a phenomenon rarely observed. Generally maturity comes only with experience and suffering. No one who has not felt the crushing weight of the Rutherford atmosphere could have painted such a vivid and life-like picture.

The basic theme in "Rutherford and Son" is not novel. Turgenev, Ibsen and such lesser artists as Sudermann and Stanley Houghton have dealt with it: the chasm between the old and the young,—the tragic struggle of parents against their children, the one frantically holding on, the other recklessly letting go. But "Rutherford and Son" is more than that. It is a picture of the paralyzing effect of tradition and institutionalism on all human life, growth, and change.

John Rutherford, the owner of the firm "Rutherford and Son," is possessed by the phantom of the past—the thing handed down to him by his father and which he must pass on to his son with undiminished luster; the thing that has turned his soul to iron and his heart to stone; the thing for the sake of which he has never known joy and because of which no one else must know joy,—"Rutherford and Son."

The crushing weight of this inexorable monster on Rutherford and his children is significantly summed up by young John:

> *John.* Have you ever heard of Moloch? No. . . . Well, Moloch was a sort of a God . . . some time ago, you know, before Dick and his kind came along. They built his image with an ugly head ten times the size of a real head, with great wheels instead of legs, and set him up in the middle of a great dirty town. And they thought him a very important person indeed, and made sacrifices to him . . . human sacrifices . . . to keep him going, you know. Out of every family they set aside one child to be an offering to him when it was big enough, and at last it became a sort of honor to be dedicated in this way, so much so, that the victims came themselves gladly to be crushed out of life under the great wheels. That was Moloch.
>
> *Janet.* Dedicated—we are dedicated—all of us—to Rutherfords'.

Not only the Rutherford children, their withered *Aunt Ann,* and old *Rutherford* himself, but even *Martin,* the faithful servant in the employ of the Rutherfords for twenty-five years, is "dedicated," and when he ceases to be of use to their Moloch, he is turned into a thief and then cast off, even as *Janet* and *John.*

Not love for *John,* his oldest son, or sympathy with the latter's wife and child induces old *Rutherford* to forgive his son's marriage with a mere shopgirl, but because he needs *John* to serve the house of Rutherford. The one inexorable purpose, always and ever!

His second son *Richard,* who is in the ministry, and "of no use" to old *Rutherford's* God of stone, receives the loving assurance: "You were no good for my purpose, and there's the end; for the matter o' that, you might just as well never ha' been born."

For that matter, his daughter *Janet* might also never have been born, except that she was "good enough" to look after her father's house, serve him, even helping take off his boots, and submitting without a murmur to the loveless, dismal life in the Rutherford home. Her father has sternly kept every suitor away, "because no one in Grantley's good enough for us." *Janet* has become faded, sour and miserable with yearning for love, for sunshine and warmth, and when she at last dares to partake of it secretly with her father's trusted man *Martin,* old *Rutherford* sets his iron heel upon her love, and drags it through the mud till it lies dead.

Again, when he faces the spirit of rebellion in his son *John, Rutherford* crushes it without the slightest hesitation in behalf of his one obsession, his one God—the House of Rutherford.

John has made an invention which holds great possibilities. By means of it he hopes to shake off the deadly grip of the Rutherfords'. He wants to become a free man and mold a new life for himself, for his wife and child. He knows his father will not credit the value of his invention. He dare not approach him: the Rutherford children have been held in dread of their parent too long.

John turns to *Martin,* the faithful servant, the only one in the confidence of *Rutherford. John* feels himself safe with *Martin.* But he does not know that *Martin,* too, is dedicated to Moloch, broken by his twenty-five years of service, left without will, without purpose outside of the Rutherfords'.

Martin tries to enlist *Rutherford's* interest in behalf of *John.* But the old man decides that *John* must turn over his invention to the House of Rutherford.

Rutherford. What's your receipt?

John. I want to know where I stand. . . . I want my price.

Rutherford. Your price—your price? Damn you impudence, sir. . . . So that's your line, is it? . . . This is what I get for all I've done for you. . . . This is the result of the schooling I gave you. I've toiled and sweated to give you a name you'd be proud to own—worked early and late, toiled like a dog when other men were taking their ease—plotted and planned to get my chance, taken it and held it when it come till I could ha' burst with the struggle. Sell! You talk o' selling to me, when everything you'll ever make couldn't pay back the life I've given to you!

John. Oh, I know, I know. I've been both for five years. Only I've had no salary.

Rutherford. You've been put to learn your business like any other young fellow. I began at the bottom—you've got to do the same. . . . Your father has lived here, and your grandfather before you. It's your inheritance—can't you realize that?—what you've got to come to when I'm under ground. We've made it for you, stone by stone, penny by penny, fighting through thick and thin for close on a hundred years. . . . It's what you've got to do—or starve. You're my son—you've got to come after me.

Janet knows her father better than *John;* she knows that "no one ever stands out against father for long—or else they get so knocked about, they don't matter any more." *Janet* knows, and when the moment arrives that brings her father's blow upon her head, it does not come as a surprise to her. When old *Rutherford* discovers her relation with *Martin,* his indignation is as characteristic of the man as everything else in his life. It is not outraged morality or a father's love. It is always and forever the House of Rutherford. Moreover, the discovery of the affair between his daughter and his workman comes at a psychologic moment: *Rutherford* is determined to get hold of *John's* invention—for the Rutherfords, of course—and now that *Martin* has broken faith with his master, his offense serves an easy pretext for *Rutherford* to break faith with *Martin.* He calls the old servant to his office and demands the receipt of *John's* invention, entrusted to *Martin.* On the latter's refusal to betray *John,* the master plays on the man's loyalty to the Rutherfords.

Rutherford. Rutherfords' is going down—down. I got to pull her up, somehow. There's one way out. . . . Mr. John's made this metal—a thing, I take your word for it, that's worth a fortune. And we're going to sit by and watch him fooling it away—selling it for a song to Miles or Jarvis, that we could break tomorrow if we had half a chance. . . . You've got but to put your hand in your pocket to save the place and you don't do it. You're with them—you're with the money-grubbing little souls that can't see beyond the next shilling they put in their pockets. . . . When men steal, Martin, they do it to gain something. If I steal this, what'll I gain by it? If I make money, what'll I buy with it? Pleasure, maybe? Children to come after me—glad o' what I done? Tell me anything in the wide world that'd bring me joy, and I'll swear to you never to touch it. . . . If you give it to me what'll you gain by it? Not a farthing shall you ever have from me—no more than I get myself.

Martin. And what will Mr. John get for it?

Rutherford. Rutherfords'—when I'm gone. He'll thank you in ten years—he'll come to laugh at himself—him and his price. He'll see the Big Thing one day, mebbe, like what I've done. He'll see that it was no more his than 'twas yours to give nor mine to take. . . . It's Rutherfords'. . . . Will you give it to me?

Martin. I take shame to be doing it now. . . . He worked it out along o' me. Every time it changed he come running to show me like a bairn wi' a new toy.

Rutherford. It's for Rutherfords'. . . .

Rutherfords' ruthlessly marches on. If the Rutherford purpose does not shrink from corrupting its most trusted servant, it surely will not bend before a daughter who has dared, even once in her life, to assert herself.

Rutherford. How far's it gone?

Janet. Right at first—I made up my mind that if you ever found out, I'd go right away, to put things straight. He wanted to tell you at the first. But I knew that it would be no use. . . . It was *I* said not to tell you.

Rutherford. Martin . . . that I trusted as I trust myself.

Janet. You haven't turned him away—you couldn't do that!

Rutherford. That's my business.

Janet. You couldn't do that . . . not Martin. . . .

Rutherford. Leave it—leave it . . . Martin's my servant, that I pay wages to. I made a name for my children—a name respected in all the countryside—and you go with a workingman. . . . To-morrow you leave my house. D'ye understand? I'll have no light ways under my roof. No one shall say I winked at it. You can bide the night. To-morrow when I come in I'm to find ye gone. . . . Your name shan't be spoken in my house . . . never again.

Janet. Oh, you've no pity. . . . I was thirty-six. Gone sour. Nobody'd ever come after me. Not even when I was young. You took care o' that. Half of my life was gone, well-nigh all of it that mattered. . . . Martin loves me honest. Don't you come near! Don't you touch that! . . . You think that I'm sorry you've found out—you think you've done for me when you use shameful words on me and turn me out o' your house. You've let me out o' jail! Whatever happens to me now, I shan't go on living as I lived here. Whatever Martin's done, he's taken me from you. You've ruined my life, you with your getting on. I've loved in wretchedness, all the joy I ever had made wicked by the fear o' you. . . . Who are you? Who are you? A man—a man that takes power to himself, power to gather people to him and use them as he wills—a man that'd take the blood of life itself and put it into the Works—into Rutherfords'. And what ha' you got by it—what? You've got Dick, that you've bullied till he's a fool—John, that's waiting for the time when he can sell what you've done—and you got me— me to take your boots off at night—to well-nigh wish you dead when I had to touch you. . . . Now! . . . Now you know it!

But for the great love in her heart, *Janet* could not have found courage to face her father as she did. But love gives strength; it instills hope and faith, and kindles anew the fires of life. Why, then, should it not be strong enough to break the fetters of even Rutherfords'? Such a love only those famished for affection and warmth can feel and *Janet* was famished for life.

Janet. I had a dream—a dream that I was in a place wi' flowers, in the summer-time, white and thick like they never grow on the moor—but it was the moor—a place near Martin's cottage. And I dreamt that he came to me with the look he had when I was a little lass, with his head up and the lie gone out of his eyes. All the time I knew I was on my bed in my room here—but it was as if sweetness poured into me, spreading and covering me like the water in the tarn when the rains are heavy in the fells. . . . That's why I dreamt of him so last night. It was as if all that was best in me was in that dream—what I was as a bairn and what I'm going to be. He couldn't help but love me. It was a message—I couldn't have thought of it by myself. It's something that's come to me—here *(putting her hands on her breast).* Part of me!

All that lay dormant in *Janet* now turns into glowing fire at the touch of Spring. But in *Martin* life has been marred, strangled by the iron hand of Rutherfords'.

Martin. Turned away I am, sure enough. Twenty-five years. And in a minute it's broke. Wi' two words.

Janet. You say that now because your heart's cold with the trouble. But it'll warm again—it'll warm again. I'll warm it out of my own heart, Martin—my heart that can't be made cold.

Martin. I'd rather ha' died than he turn me away. I'd ha' lost everything in the world to know that I was true to 'm, like I was till you looked at me wi' the love in your face. It was a great love ye gave me—you in your grand hoose wi' your delicate ways. But it's broke me.

Janet. But—it's just the same with us. Just the same as ever it was.

Martin. Aye. But there's no mending, wi' the likes o' him.

Janet. What's there to mend? What's there to mend except what's bound you like a slave all the years? You're free—free for the first time since you were a lad mebbe. We'll begin again. We'll be happy—happy. You and me, free in the world! All the time that's been 'll be just like a dream that's past, a waiting time afore we found each other—the long winter afore the flowers come out white and thick on the moors—

Martin. Twenty-five years ago he took me.... It's too long to change.
... I'll never do his work no more; but it's like as if he'd be my master just the
same—all I die—

Janet. Listen, Martin. Listen to me. You've worked all your life for him, ever
since you were a little lad. Early and late you've been at the Works—
working—working—for him.

Martin. Gladly!

Janet. Now and then he give you a kind word—when you were wearied out
mebbe—and your thoughts might ha' turned to what other men's lives were, wi'
time for rest and pleasure. You didn't see through him, you wi' your big heart,
Martin. You were too near to see, like I was till Mary came. You worked gladly
maybe—but all the time your life was going into Rutherfords'—your manhood
into the place he's built. He's had you, Martin,—like he's had me, and all of us.
We used to say he was hard and ill-tempered. Bad to do with in the house—we
fell silent when he came in—we couldn't see for the little things,—we couldn't see
the years passing because of the days. And all the time it was our lives he was
taking bit by bit—our lives that we'll never get back.... Now's our chance at
last! He's turned us both away, me as well as you. We two he's sent out into the
world together. Free. He's done it himself of his own will. It's ours to take,
Martin—our happiness. We'll get it in spite of him. He'd kill it if he could.

The cruelty of it, that the Rutherfords never kill with one blow: never so
merciful are they. In their ruthless march they strangle inch by inch, shed the
blood of life drop by drop, until they have broken the very spirit of man and
made him as helpless and pitiful as *Martin,*—a trembling leaf tossed about by
the winds.

A picture of such stirring social and human importance that no one, except
he who has reached the stage of *Martin,* can escape its effect. Yet even more
significant is the inevitability of the doom of the Rutherfords as embodied in
the wisdom of *Mary, John's* wife.

When her husband steals his father's money—a very small part indeed
compared with what the father had stolen from him—he leaves the hateful
place and *Mary* remains to face the master. For the sake of her child she
strikes a bargain with *Rutherford.*

Mary. A bargain is where one person has something to sell that another wants
to buy. There's no love in it—only money—money that pays for life. I've got
something to sell that you want to buy.

Rutherford. What's that?

Mary. My son. You've lost everything you've had in the world. John's gone—and Richard—and Janet. They won't come back. You're alone now and getting old, with no one to come after you. When you die Rutherfords' will be sold—somebody'll buy it and give it a new name perhaps, and no one will even remember that you made it. That'll be the end of all your work. Just—nothing. You've thought of that. . . . It's for my boy. I want—a chance of life for him—his place in the world. John can't give him that, because he's made so. If I went to London and worked my hardest I'd get twenty-five shillings a week. We've failed. From you I can get when I want for my boy. I want—all the good common things: a good house, good food, warmth. He's a delicate little thing now, but he'll grow strong like other children. . . . Give me what I ask, and in return I'll give you—him. On one condition. I'm to stay on here. I won't trouble you—you needn't speak to me or see me unless you want to. For ten years he's to be absolutely mine, to do what I like with. You mustn't interfere—you mustn't tell him to do things or frighten him. He's mine for ten years more.

Rutherford. And after that?

Mary. He'll be yours.

Rutherford. To train up. For Rutherfords'?

Mary. Yes.

Rutherford. After all? After Dick, that I've bullied till he's a fool? John, that's wished me dead?

Mary. In ten years you'll be an old man; you won't be able to make people afraid of you any more.

When I saw the masterly presentation of the play on the stage, *Mary's* bargain looked unreal and incongruous. It seemed impossible to me that a mother who really loves her child should want it to be in any way connected with the Rutherfords'. But after repeatedly rereading the play, I was convinced by Mary's simple statement: "In ten years you'll be an old man; you won't be able to make people afraid of you any more." Most deeply true. The Rutherfords are bound by time, by the eternal forces of change. Their influence on human life is indeed terrible. Notwithstanding it all, however, they are fighting a losing game. They are growing old, already too old to make anyone afraid. Change and innovation are marching on, and the Rutherfords must make place for the young generation knocking at the gates.

THE IRISH DRAMA

WILLIAM BUTLER YEATS

Most Americans know about the Irish people only that they are not averse to drink, and they that make brutal policemen and corrupt politicians. But those who are familiar with the revolutionary movements of the past are aware of the fortitude and courage, aye, of the heroism of the Irish, manifested during their uprisings, and especially in the Fenian movement—the people's revolt against political despotism and land robbery.

And though for years Ireland has contributed to the very worst features of American life, those interested in the fate of its people did not despair; they knew that the spirit of unrest in Ireland was not appeased, and that it would make itself felt again in no uncertain form.

The cultural and rebellious awakening in that country within the last twenty-five years once more proves that neither God nor King can for long suppress the manifestation of the latent possibilities of a people. The possibilities of the Irish must indeed be great if they could inspire the rich humor of a Lady Gregory, the deep symbolism of a Yeats, the poetic fancy of a Synge, and the rebellion of a Robinson and Murray.

Only a people unspoiled by the dulling hand of civilization and free from artifice can retain such simplicity of faith and remain so imaginative, so full of fancy and dreams, wild and fiery, which have kindled the creative spark in the Irish dramatists of our time. It is true that the work of only the younger element among them is of social significance, yet all of them have rendered their people and the rest of the world a cultural service of no mean value. William Butler Yeats is among the latter, together with Synge and Lady Gregory; his art, though deep in human appeal, has no bearing on the pressing questions of our time. Mr. Yeats himself would repudiate any implication of a social character, as he considers such dramas too "topical" and therefore "half bad" plays. In view of this attitude, it is difficult to reconcile his standard of true art with the repertoire of the Abbey Theater, which consists mainly of social dramas. Still more difficult is it to account for his work, "Where There is Nothing," which is no less social in its philosophy and tendency than Ibsen's "Brand."

WHERE THERE IS NOTHING

"Where There Is Nothing" is as true an interpretation of the philosophy of Anarchism as could be given by its best exponents. I say this not out of any wish to tag Mr. Yeats, but because the ideal of *Paul Ruttledge,* the hero of the play, is nothing less than Anarchism applied to everyday life.

Paul Ruttledge, a man of wealth, comes to the conclusion, after a long process of development and growth, that riches are wrong, and that the life of the propertied is artificial, useless and inane.

Paul Ruttledge. When I hear these people talking I always hear some organized or vested interest chirp or quack, as it does in the newspapers. I would like to have great iron claws, and to put them about the pillars, and to pull and pull till everything fell into pieces.... Sometimes I dream I am pulling down my own house, and sometimes it is the whole world that I am pulling down.... When everything was pulled down we would have more room to get drunk in, to drink contentedly out of the cup of life, out of the drunken cup of life.

He decides to give up his position and wealth and cast his lot in with the tinkers—an element we in America know as "hoboes," men who tramp the highways making their living as they go about, mending kettles and pots, earning an honest penny without obligation or responsibility to anyone.

Paul Ruttledge longs for the freedom of the road,—to sleep under the open sky, to count the stars, to be free. He throws off all artificial restraint and is received with open arms by the tinkers. To identify himself more closely with their life, he marries a tinker's daughter—not according to the rites of State or Church, but in true tinker fashion—in freedom—bound only by the promise to be faithful and "not hurt each other."

In honor of the occasion, *Paul* tenders to his comrades and the people of the neighborhood a grand feast, full of the spirit of life's joy,—an outpouring of gladness that lasts a whole week.

Paul's brother, his friends, and the authorities are incensed over the carousal. They demand that he terminate the "drunken orgy."

Mr. Joyce. This is a disgraceful business, Paul; the whole countryside is demoralized. There is not a man who has come to sensible years who is not drunk.

Mr. Dowler. This is a flagrant violation of all propriety. Society is shaken to its roots. My own servants have been led astray by the free drinks that are being given in the village. My butler, who has been with me for seven years, has not been seen for the last two days.

Mr. Algie. I endorse his sentiments completely. There has not been a stroke of work done for the last week. The hay is lying in ridges where it has been cut, there is not a man to be found to water the cattle. It is impossible to get as much as a horse shod in the village.

Paul Ruttledge. I think *you* have something to say, Colonel Lawley?

Colonel Lawley. I have undoubtedly. I want to know when law and order are to be reëstablished. The police have been quite unable to cope with the disorder. Some of them have themselves got drunk. If my advice had been taken the military would have been called in.

Mr. Green. The military are not indispensable on occasions like the present. There are plenty of police coming now. We have wired to Dublin for them, they will be here by the four o'clock train.

Paul Ruttledge. But you have not told me what you have come here for. Is there anything I can do for you?

Mr. Green. We have come to request you to go to the public-houses, to stop the free drinks, to send the people back to their work. As for those tinkers, the law will deal with them when the police arrive.

Paul Ruttledge. I wanted to give a little pleasure to my fellow-creatures.

Mr. Dowler. This seems rather a low form of pleasure.

Paul Ruttledge. I daresay it seems to you a little violent. But the poor have very few hours in which to enjoy themselves; they must take their pleasure raw; they haven't the time to cook it. Have we not tried sobriety? Do you like it? I found it very dull. . . . Think what it is to them to have their imagination like a blazing tar-barrel for a whole week. Work could never bring them such blessedness as that.

Mr. Dowler. Everyone knows there is no more valuable blessing than work.

Paul Ruttledge decides to put his visitors "on trial," to let them see themselves as they are in all their hypocrisy, all their corruption.

He charges the military man, *Colonel Lawley,* with calling himself a Christian, yet following the business of man-killing. The Colonel is forced to admit that he had ordered his men to fight in a war, of the justice of which they knew nothing, or did not believe in, and yet it is "the doctrine of your Christian church, of your Catholic church, that he who fights in an unjust war, knowing it to be unjust, loses his own soul." Of the rich man *Dowler,*

Paul Ruttledge demands whether he could pass through the inside of a finger ring, and on *Paul's* attention being called by one of the tinkers to the fine coat of *Mr. Dowler*, he tells him to help himself to it. Threatened by *Mr. Green*, the spokesman of the law, with encouraging robbery, *Ruttledge* admonishes him.

> *Ruttledge*. Remember the commandment, "Give to him that asketh thee"; and the hard commandment goes even farther, "Him that taketh thy cloak forbid not to take thy coat also."

But the worst indictment *Ruttledge* hurls against *Mr. Green*. The other professed Christians kill, murder, do not love their enemies, and do not give to any man that asks of them. But the Greens, *Ruttledge* says, are the worst of all. For the others break the law of Christ for their own pleasure, but "you take pay for breaking it; when their goods are taken away you condemn the taker; when they are smitten on one cheek you punish the smiter. You encourage them in their breaking of the Law of Christ."

For several years *Ruttledge* lives the life of the tinkers. But of weak physique, he finds himself unable to withstand the rigors of the road. His health breaks down, and his faithful comrades carry him to his native town and bring him to a monastery where *Paul* is cared for by the priests. While there he begins to preach a wonderful gospel, a gospel strange to the friars and the superior,—so rebellious and terrible that he is declared a dissenter, a heathen and a dangerous character.

> *Paul Ruttledge*. Now I can give you the message that has come to me. . . . Lay down your palm branches before this altar; you have brought them as a sign that the walls are beginning to be broken up, that we are going back to the joy of the green earth. . . . For a long time after their making men and women wandered here and there, half blind from the drunkenness of Eternity; they had not yet forgotten that the green Earth was the Love of God, and that all Life was the Will of God, and so they wept and laughed and hated according to the impulse of their hearts. They gathered the great Earth to their breasts and their lips, . . . in what they believed would be an eternal kiss. It was then that the temptation began. The men and women listened to them, and because when they had lived . . . in mother wit and natural kindness, they sometimes did one another an injury, they thought that it would be better to be safe than to be blessed, they made the Laws. The Laws were the first sin. They were the first mouthful of the apple; the moment man had made them he began to die; we must put out the Laws as I put

Laws as I put out this candle. And when they had lived amidst the green Earth that is the Love of God, they were sometimes wetted by the rain, and sometimes cold and hungry, and sometimes alone from one another; they thought it would be better to be comfortable than to be blessed. They began to build big houses and big towns. They grew wealthy and they sat chattering at their doors; and the embrace that was to have been eternal ended. . . . We must put out the towns as I put out this candle. But that is not all, for man created a worse thing. . . . Man built up the Church. We must destroy the Church, we must put it out as I put out this candle. . . . We must destroy everything that has Law and Number.

The rebel is driven from the monastery. He is followed by only two faithful friars, his disciples, who go among the people to disseminate the new gospel. But the people fail to understand them. Immersed in darkness and superstition, they look upon these strange men as evildoers. They accuse them of casting an evil spell on their cattle and disturbing the people's peace. The path of the crusader is thorny, and *Colman,* the friar disciple of *Paul,* though faithful for a time, becomes discouraged in the face of opposition and persecution. He weakens.

Colman. It's no use stopping waiting for the wind; if we have anything to say that's worth the people listening to, we must bring them to hear it one way or another. Now, it is what I was saying to Aloysius, we must begin teaching them to make things, they never had the chance of any instruction of this sort here. Those and other things, we got a good training in the old days. And we'll get a grant from the Technical Board. The Board pays up to four hundred pounds to some of its instructors.

Paul Ruttledge. Oh, I understand; you will sell them. And what about the dividing of the money? You will need to make laws about that. Oh, we will grow quite rich in time.

Colman. We'll build workshops and houses for those who come to work from a distance, good houses, slated, not thatched. . . . They will think so much more of our teaching when we have got them under our influence by other things. Of course we will teach them their meditations, and give them a regular religious life. We must settle out some little place for them to pray in—there's a high gable over there where we could hang a bell—

Paul Ruttledge. Oh, yes, I understand. You would weave them together like this, you would add one thing to another, laws and money and church and bells, till you had got everything back again that you had escaped from. But it is my business to tear things asunder.

Aloysius. Brother Paul, it is what I am thinking; now the tinkers have come back to you, you could begin to gather a sort of an army; you can't fight your battle without an army. They would call to the other tinkers, and the tramps and the beggars, and the sieve-makers and all the wandering people. It would be a great army.

Paul Ruttledge. Yes, that would be a great army, a great wandering army.

Aloysius. The people would be afraid to refuse us then; we would march on—

Paul Ruttledge. We could march on. We could march on the towns, and we could break up all settled order; we could bring back the old joyful, dangerous, individual life. We would have banners. We will have one great banner that will go in front, it will take two men to carry it, and on it we will have Laughter—

Aloysius. That will be the banner for the front. We will have different troops, we will have captains to organize them, to give them orders.

Paul Ruttledge. To organize? That is to bring in law and number. Organize—organize—that is how all the mischief has been done. I was forgetting,—we cannot destroy the world with armies; it is inside our minds that it must be destroyed.

Deserted, *Paul Ruttledge* stands alone in his crusade, like most iconoclasts. Misunderstood and persecuted, he finally meets his death at the hands of the infuriated mob.

"Where There Is Nothing" is of great social significance, deeply revolutionary in the sense that it carries the message of the destruction of every institution—State, Property, and Church—that enslaves humanity. *For where there is nothing, there man begins.*

A certain critic characterized this play as a "statement of revolt against the despotism of facts." Is there a despotism more compelling and destructive than that of the facts of property, of the State and Church? But "Where There Is Nothing" is not merely a "statement" of revolt. It embodies the spirit of revolt itself, of that most constructive revolt which begins with the destruction of every obstacle in the path of the new life that is to grow on the débris of the old, when the paralyzing yoke of institutionalism shall have been broken, and man left free to enjoy Life and Laughter.

LENOX ROBINSON

HARVEST

Timothy Hurley, an old farmer, slaves all his life and mortgages his farm in order to enable his children to lead an idle, parasitic life.

Started on this road toward so-called culture by the school-master, *William Lordan, Hurley's* children leave their father's farm and in due time establish themselves in society as priest, lawyer, secretary and chemist, respectively.

The secretary son is ashamed of his lowly origin and denies it. The lawyer son is much more concerned with his motor car than with the condition of the farm that has helped him on his feet. The priest has departed for America, there to collect funds for Church work. Only *Maurice,* the youngest son of *Timothy Hurley,* remains at home as the farm drudge, the typical man with the hoe.

Jack Hurley, the chemist, and *Timothy's* only daughter *Mary*, retain some loyalty to the old place, but when they return after an absence of years, they find themselves out of touch with farm life, and they too turn their back on their native heath. *Jack Hurley's* notion of the country is that of most city people: nature is beautiful, the scenery lovely, so long as it is someone else who has to labor in the scorching sun, to plow and toil in the sweat of his brow.

Jack and his wife *Mildred* are both extremely romantic about the farm.

Jack. It stands to reason farming must pay enormously. Take a field of oats, for instance; every grain that's sown gives a huge percentage in return.... I don't know exactly how many grains a stalk carries, but several hundred I'm sure ... why, there's no investment in the world would give you a return like that.

But soon they discover that every grain of corn does not yield hundreds of dollars.

Maurice. You can't have a solicitor, and a priest, and a chemist in a family without spending money, and for the last ten years you've been all drawing money out of the farm ... there's no more to drain now.... Oh, I suppose you think I'm a bloody fool not to be able to make it pay; but sure what chance have I

144

and I never taught how to farm? There was money and education wanted to make priests and doctors and gentlemen of you all, and wasn't there money an' education wanted to make a farmer of me? No; nothing taught me only what I picked up from my father and the men, and never a bit of fresh money to put into the farm only it all kept to make a solicitor of Bob and a chemist of you.

During *Jack's* visit to the farm a fire breaks out and several buildings on the place are destroyed. Much to the horror of the well-bred *Jack,* he learns that his father himself had lit the match in order to get "compensation." He sternly upbraids the old farmer.

Jack. Didn't you see yourself how dishonest it was?

Timothy. Maybe I did, but I saw something more, and that was that I was on the way to being put out of the farm.

Jack is outraged; he threatens to inform on his own people and offers to stay on the farm to help with the work. But two weeks' experience in the field beneath the burning sun is more than delicate *Jack* can stand. He suffers fainting spells, and is in the end prevailed upon by his wife to leave.

Mary, old *Hurley's* daughter, also returns to the farm for rest and quiet. But she finds no peace there, for the city is too much in her blood. There is, moreover, another lure she cannot escape.

Mary. I was too well educated to be a servant, and I was never happy as one, so to better myself I learned typing. . . . It's a hard life, Jack, and I soon found out how hard it was, and I was as dissatisfied as ever. Then there only seemed one way out of it . . . and he . . . my employer, I mean. . . . I went into it deliberately with my eyes open. You see, a woman I knew chucked typing and went in for this . . . and I saw what a splendid time she had, and how happy she was—and I was so miserably unhappy—and how she had everything she wanted and I had nothing, and . . . and . . . But this life made me unhappy, too, and so in desperation I came home; but I've grown too far away from it all, and now I'm going back. Don't you see, Jack, I'm not happy here. I thought if I could get home to the farm and the old simple life it would be all right, but it isn't. Everything jars on me, the roughness and the hard living and the coarse food—oh, it seems ridiculous—but they make me physically ill. I always thought, if I could get away home to Knockmalgloss I could start fair again. . . . So I came home, and everything is the same, and everyone thinks that I'm as pure and innocent as when I went away, but . . . but . . . But, Jack, the dreadful thing is I want to go back. . . . I'm longing for that life, and its excitement and splendor and color.

In her misery and struggle a great faith sustains *Mary* and keeps her from ruin. It is the thought of her father, in whom she believes implicitly as her ideal of honesty, strength and incorruptibility. The shock is terrible when she learns that her father, even her father, has fallen a victim to the cruel struggle of life,—that her father himself set fire to the buildings.

Mary. And I thought he was so simple, so innocent, so unspoiled! ... Father, the simple, honest peasant, the only decent one of us. I cried all last night at the contrast! His unselfishness, his simplicity.... Why, we're all equally bad now—he and I—we both sell ourselves, he for the price of those old houses and I for a few years of splendor and happiness....

The only one whom life seems to teach nothing is *Schoolmaster Lordan*. Oblivious of the stress and storm of reality, he continues to be enraptured with education, with culture, with the opportunities offered by the large cities. He is particularly proud of the Hurley children.

Lordan. The way you've all got on! I tell you what, if every boy and girl I ever taught had turned out a failure I'd feel content and satisfied when I looked at all of you and saw what I've made of you.

Mary. What you've made of us? I wonder do you really know what you've made of us?

Lordan. Isn't it easily seen? One with a motor car, no less. ... It was good, sound seed I sowed long ago in the little schoolhouse and it's to-day you're all reaping the harvest.

"Harvest" is a grim picture of civilization in its especially demoralizing effects upon the people who spring from the soil. The mock culture and shallow education which inspire peasant folk with awe, which lure the children away from home, only to crush the vitality out of them or to turn them into cowards and compromisers. The tragedy of a civilization that dooms the tillers of the soil to a dreary monotony of hard toil with little return, or charms them to destruction with the false glow of city culture and ease! Greater still this tragedy in a country like Ireland, its people taxed to the very marrow and exploited to the verge of starvation, leaving the young generation no opening, no opportunity in life.

It is inevitable that the sons and daughters of Ireland, robust in body and spirit, yearning for things better and bigger, should desert her. For as *Mary* says, "When the sun sets here, it's all so dark and cold and dreary." But the young need light and warmth—and these are not in the valley of ever-present misery and want.

"Harvest" is an expressive picture of the social background of the Irish people, a background somber and unpromising but for the streak of dawn that pierces that country's dark horizon in the form of the inherent and irrepressible fighting spirit of the true Irishman, the spirit of the Fenian revolt whose fires often slumber but are never put out, all the ravages of our false civilization notwithstanding.

T. G. MURRAY

MAURICE HARTE

"Maurice Harte" portrays the most sinister force which holds the Irish people in awe—that heaviest of all bondage, priestcraft.

Michael Harte, his wife *Ellen,* and their son *Owen* are bent on one purpose; to make a priest of their youngest child *Maurice.* The mother especially has no other ambition in life than to see her son "priested." No higher ideal to most Catholic mothers than to consecrate their favorite son to the glory of God.

What it has cost the Hartes to attain their ambition and hope is revealed by *Ellen Harte* in the conversation with her sister and later with her husband, when he informs her that he cannot borrow any more money to continue the boy in the seminary.

Mrs. Harte. If Michael and myself have our son nearly a priest this day, 'tis no small price at all we have paid for it. . . . Isn't it the terrible thing, every time you look through that window, to have the fear in your heart that 'tis the process-server you'll see and he coming up the boreen?

Old Harte impoverishes himself to enable his son to finish his studies. He has borrowed right and left, till his resources are now entirely exhausted. But he is compelled to try another loan.

Michael. He made out 'twas as good as insulting him making such a small payment, and the money that's on us to be so heavy. "If you don't wish to sign that note," says he, "you needn't. It don't matter at all to me one way or the other, for before the next Quarter Sessions 'tis Andy Driscoll, the process-server, will be marching up to your door." So what could I do but sign? Why, 'twas how he turned on me in a red passion. "And isn't it a scandal, Michael Harte," says he, "for the like o' you, with your name on them books there for a hundred and fifty pounds, and you with only the grass of nine or ten cows, to be making your son a priest? The like of it," says he, "was never heard of before."

Mrs. Harte. What business was it of his, I'd like to know? Jealous of us! There's no fear any of his sons will ever be anything much!

Michael. I was thinking it might do Maurice some harm with the Bishop if it came out on the papers that we were up before the judge for a civil bill.

Mrs. Harte. ... 'Tisn't once or twice I told you that I had my heart set on hearing Maurice say the marriage words over his own brother.

Maurice comes home for the summer vacation, looking pale and emaciated. His mother ascribes his condition to the bad city air and hard study at school. But *Maurice* suffers from a different cause. His is a mental struggle: the maddening struggle of doubt, the realization that he has lost his faith, that he has no vocation, and that he must give up his divinity studies. He knows how fanatically bent his people are on having him ordained, and he is tortured by the grief his decision will cause his parents. His heart is breaking as he at last determines to inform them.

He reasons and pleads with his parents and implores them not to drive him back to college. But they cannot understand. They remain deaf to his arguments; pitifully they beg him not to fail them, not to disappoint the hope of a lifetime. When it all proves of no avail, they finally disclose to *Maurice* their gnawing secret: the farm has been mortgaged and many debts incurred for the sake of enabling him to attain to the priesthood.

Michael. Maurice, would you break our hearts?

Maurice. Father, would you have your son live a life of sacrilege? Would you, Father? Would you?

Mrs. Harte. That's only foolish talk, Aren't you every bit as good as the next?

Maurice. I may be, but I haven't a vocation. ... My mind is finally made up.

Mrs. Harte. Maurice, listen to me—listen to me! ... If it went out about you this day, isn't it destroyed forever we'd be? Look! The story wouldn't be east in Macroom when we'd have the bailiffs walking in that door. The whole world knows he is to be priested next June, and only for the great respect they have for us through the means o' that, 'tisn't James McCarthy alone, but every other one o' them would come down on us straight for their money. In one week there wouldn't be a cow left by us, nor a horse, nor a lamb, nor anything at all! ... Look at them books. 'Tis about time you should know how we stand here. ... God knows, I wouldn't be hard on you at all, but look at the great load o' money that's on us this day, and mostly all on your account.

Maurice. Mother, don't make my cross harder to bear.

Mrs. Harte. An' would you be seeing a heavier cross put on them that did all that mortal man and woman could do for you?

Maurice. Look! I'll wear the flesh off my bones, but in pity spare me!

Mrs. Harte. And will you have no pity at all on us and on Owen here, that have slaved for you all our lives?

Maurice. Mother! Mother!

Mrs. Harte. You'll go back? 'Tis only a mistake?

Maurice. Great God of Heaven! . . . you'll kill me.

Michael. You'll go back, Maurice? The vocation will come to you in time with the help of God. It will, surely.

Maurice. Don't ask me! Don't ask me!

Mrs. Harte. If you don't how can I ever face outside this door or lift my head again? . . . How could I listen to the neighbors making pity for me, and many a one o' them only glad in their hearts? How could I ever face again into town o' Macroom?

Maurice. Oh, don't.

Mrs. Harte. I tell you, Maurice, I'd rather be lying dead a thousand times in the graveyard over Killnamartyra—

Maurice. Stop, Mother, stop! I'll—I'll go back—as—as you all wish it.

Nine months later there is general rejoicing at the Hartes': *Maurice* has passed his examinations with flying colors; he is about to be ordained, and he is to officiate at the wedding of his brother *Owen* and his wealthy bride.

Ellen Harte plans to give her son a royal welcome. Great preparations are on foot to greet the return of *Maurice.* He comes back—not in the glory and triumph expected by his people, but a driveling idiot. His mental struggle, the agony of whipping himself to the hated task, proved too much for him, and *Maurice* is sacrificed on the altar of superstition and submission to paternal authority.

In the whole range of the Irish drama "Maurice Harte" is the most Irish, because nowhere does Catholicism demand so many victims as in that unfortunate land. But in a deeper sense the play is of that social importance that knows no limit of race or creed.

There is no boundary of land or time to the resistance of the human mind to coercion; it is world-wide. Equally so is the rebellion of youth against the tyranny of parents. But above all does this play mirror the self-centered, narrow, ambitious love of the mother, so disastrous to the happiness and peace of her child. For it is *Ellen Harte,* rather than the father, who forces *Maurice* back to his studies. From whatever viewpoint, however, "Maurice Harte" be considered, it carries a dramatically powerful message of wide social significance.

THE RUSSIAN DRAMA

People outside of Russia, especially Anglo-Saxons, have one great objection to the Russian drama: it is too sad, too gloomy. It is often asked, "Why is the Russian drama so pessimistic?" The answer is: the Russian drama, like all Russian culture, has been conceived in the sorrow of the people; it was born in their woe and struggle. Anything thus conceived cannot be very joyous or amusing.

It is no exaggeration to say that in no other country are the creative artists so interwoven, so much at one with the people. This is not only true of men like Turgenev, Tolstoy and the dramatists of modern times. It applies also to Gogol, who in "The Inspector" and "Dead Souls" spoke in behalf of the people, appealing to the conscience of Russia. The same is true of Dostoyevsky, of the poets Nekrassov, Nadson, and others. In fact, all the great Russian artists have gone to the people for their inspiration, as to the source of all life. That explains the depth and the humanity of Russian literature.

The modern drama naturally suggests Henrik Ibsen as its pioneer. But prior to him, Gogol utilized the drama as a vehicle for popularizing the social issues of his time. In "The Inspector," *(Revizor)* he portrays the corruption, graft and extortion rampant in the governmental departments. If we were to Anglicize the names of the characters in "The Inspector," and forget for a moment that it was a Russian who wrote the play, the criticism contained therein would apply with similar force to present-day America, and to every other modern country. Gogol touched the deepest sores of social magnitude and marked the beginning of the realistic drama in Russia.

However, it is not within the scope of this work to discuss the drama of Gogol's era. I shall begin with Tolstoy, because he is closer to our own generation, and voices more definitely the social significance of the modern drama.

TOLSTOY

When Leo Tolstoy died, the representatives of the Church proclaimed him as their own. "He was with us," they said. It reminds one of the Russian fable about the fly and the ox. The fly was lazily resting on the horn of the ox while he plowed the field, but when the ox returned home exhausted with toil, the fly bragged, "*We* have been plowing." The spokesmen of the Church are, in relation to Tolstoy, in the same position. It is true that Tolstoy based his conception of human relationships on a new interpretation of the Gospels. But he was as far removed from present-day Christianity as Jesus was alien to the institutional religion of his time.

Tolstoy was the last true Christian, and as such he undermined the stronghold of the Church with all its pernicious power of darkness, with all its injustice and cruelty.

For this he was persecuted by the Holy Synod and excommunicated from the Church; for this he was feared by the Tsar and his henchmen; for this his works have been condemned and prohibited.

The only reason Tolstoy himself escaped the fate of other great Russians was that he was mightier than the Church, mightier than the ducal clique, mightier even than the Tsar. He was the powerful conscience of Russia exposing her crimes and evils before the civilized world.

How deeply Tolstoy felt the grave problems of his time, how closely related he was to the people, he demonstrated in various works, but in none so strikingly as in "The Power of Darkness."

THE POWER OF DARKNESS

"The Power of Darkness" is the tragedy of sordid misery and dense ignorance. It deals with a group of peasants steeped in poverty and utter darkness. This appalling condition, especially in relation to the women folk, is expressed by one of the characters in the play:

Mitrich. There are millions of you women and girls, but you are all like the beasts of the forest. Just as one has been born, so she dies. She has neither seen or heard anything. A man will learn something; if nowhere else, at least in the inn, or by some chance, in prison, or in the army, as I have. But what about a woman? She does not know a thing about God,—nay, she does not know one day from another. They creep about like blind pups, and stick their heads into the manure.

Peter, a rich peasant, is in a dying condition. Yet he clings to his money and slave-drives his young wife, *Anisya*, his two daughters by a first marriage, and his peasant servant *Nikita*. He will not allow them any rest from their toil, for the greed of money is in his blood and the fear of death in his bones. *Anisya* hates her husband: he forces her to drudge, and he is old and ill. She loves *Nikita*. The latter, young and irresponsible, cannot resist women, who are his main weakness and final undoing. Before he came to old *Peter's* farm, he had wronged an orphan girl. When she becomes pregnant, she appeals to *Nikita's* father, *Akim*, a simple and honest peasant. He urges his son to marry the girl, because "it is a sin to wrong an orphan. Look out, Nikita! A tear of offense does not flow past, but upon a man's head. Look out, or the same will happen with you."

Akim's kindness and simplicity are opposed by the viciousness and greed of his wife *Matrena*. *Nikita* remains on the farm, and *Anisya*, urged and influenced by his mother, poisons old *Peter* and steals his money.

When her husband dies, *Anisya* marries *Nikita* and turns the money over to him. *Nikita* becomes the head of the house, and soon proves himself a rake and a tyrant. Idleness and affluence undermine whatever good is latent in him. Money, the destroyer of souls, together with the consciousness that he has been indirectly a party to *Anisya's* crime, turn *Nikita's* love for the woman into bitter hatred. He takes for his mistress *Akulina*, *Peter's* oldest daughter, a girl of sixteen, deaf and silly, and forces *Anisya* to serve them. She had strength to resist her old husband, but her love for *Nikita* has made her weak. "The moment I see him my heart softens. I have no courage against him."

Old *Akim* comes to ask for a little money from his newly rich son. He quickly senses the swamp of corruption and vice into which *Nikita* has sunk. He tries to save him, to bring him back to himself, to arouse the better side of his nature. But he fails.

The ways of life are too evil for *Akim*. He leaves, refusing even the money he needs so badly to purchase a horse.

Akim. One sin holds on to another and pulls you along. Nikita, you are stuck in sins. You are stuck, I see, in sins. You are stuck fast, so to speak. I have heard that nowadays they pull fathers' beards, so to speak,—but this leads only to ruin, to ruin, so to speak. . . . There is your money. I will go and beg, so to speak, but I will not, so to speak, take the money. . . . Let me go! I will not stay! I would rather sleep near the fence than in your nastiness.

The type of *Akim* is most vividly characterized by Tolstoy in the talk between the old peasant and the new help on the farm.

Mitrich. Let us suppose, for example, you have money, and I, for example, have my land lying fallow; it is spring, and I have no seed; or I have to pay the taxes. So I come to you, and say: "Akim, give me ten roubles! I will have the harvest in by St. Mary's Intercession and then I will give it back to you, with a tithe for the accommodation." You, for example, see that I can be flayed, having a horse or a cow, so you say: "Give me two or three roubles for the accommodation." The noose is around my neck, and I cannot get along without it. "Very well," says I, "I will take the ten roubles." In the fall I sell some things, and I bring you the money, and you skin me in addition for three roubles.

Akim. But this is, so to speak, a wrong done to a peasant. If one forgets God, so to speak, it is not good.

Mitrich. Wait a minute! So remember what you have done: you have fleeced me, so to speak, and Anisya, for example, has some money which is lying idle. She has no place to put it in and, being a woman, does not know what to do with it. So she comes to you: "Can't I," says she, "make some use of my money?" "Yes, you can," you say. And so you wait. Next summer I come to you once more. "Give me another ten roubles," says I, "and I will pay you for the accommodation." So you watch me to see whether my hide has not been turned yet, whether I can be flayed again, and if I can, you give me Anisya's money. But if I have not a blessed thing, and nothing to eat, you make your calculations, seeing that I cannot be skinned, and you say: "God be with you, my brother!" and you look out for another man to whom to give Anisya's money, and whom you can flay. Now this is called a bank. So it keeps going around. It is a very clever thing, my friend.

Akim. What is this? This is a nastiness, so to speak. If a peasant, so to speak, were to do it, the peasants would regard it as a sin, so to speak. This is not according to the Law, not according to the Law, so to speak. It is bad. How can the learned men, so to speak— . . . As I look at it, so to speak, there is trouble without money, so to speak, and with money the trouble is double, so to speak. God has commanded to work. But you put the money in the bank, so to speak, and lie down to sleep, and the money will feed you, so to speak, while you are lying. This is bad,—not according to the Law, so to speak.

Mitrich. Not according to the Law? The Law does not trouble people nowadays, my friend. All they think about is how to clean out a fellow. That's what! As long as *Akulina's* condition is not noticeable, the relation of *Nikita* with his dead master's daughter remains hidden from the neighbors. But the time comes when she is to give birth to a child. It is then that *Anisya* becomes mistress of the situation again. Her hatred for *Akulina*, her outraged love for *Nikita* and the evil spirit of *Nikita's* mother all combine to turn her into a fiend. *Akulina* is driven to the barn, where her terrible labor pains are stifled by the dread of her stepmother. When the innocent victim is born, *Nikita's* vicious mother and *Anisya* persuade him that the child is dead and force him to bury it in the cellar.

While *Nikita* is digging the grave, he discovers the deception. The child is alive! The terrible shock unnerves the man, and in temporary madness he presses a board over the little body till its bones crunch. Superstition, horror and the perfidy of the women drive *Nikita* to drink in an attempt to drown the baby's cries constantly ringing in his ears.

The last act deals with *Akulina's* wedding to the son of a neighbor. She is forced into the marriage because of her misfortune. The peasants all gather for the occasion, but *Nikita* is missing: he roams the place haunted by the horrible phantom of his murdered child. He attempts to hang himself but fails, and finally decides to go before the entire assembly to confess his crimes.

Nikita. Father, listen to me! First of all, Marina, look at me! I am guilty toward you: I had promised to marry you, and I seduced you. I deceived you and abandoned you; forgive me for Christ's sake!

Matrena. Oh, oh, he is bewitched. What is the matter with him? He has the evil eye upon him. Get up and stop talking nonsense!

Nikita. I killed your father, and I, dog, have ruined his daughter. I had the power over her, and I killed also her baby. . . . Father dear! Forgive me, sinful man! You told me, when I first started on this life of debauch: "When the claw is caught, the whole bird is lost." But, I, dog, did not pay any attention to you, and so everything turned out as you said. Forgive me, for Christ's sake.

The "Power of Darkness" is a terrible picture of poverty, ignorance and superstition. To write such a work it is not sufficient to be a creative artist: it requires a deeply sympathetic human soul. Tolstoy possessed both. He understood that the tragedy of the peasants' life is due not to any inherent viciousness but to the power of darkness which permeates their existence from the cradle to the grave. Something heavy is oppressing them—in the words of *Anisya*—weighing them down, something that saps all humanity out of them and drives them into the depths.

"The Power of Darkness" is a social picture at once appalling and gripping.

ANTON CHEKHOV

When Anton Chekhov first came to the fore, no less an authority than Tolstoy said: "Russia has given birth to another Turgenev." The estimate was not overdrawn. Chekhov was indeed a modern Turgenev. Perhaps not as universal, because Turgenev, having lived in western Europe, in close contact with conditions outside of Russia, dealt with more variegated aspects of life. But as a creative artist Chekhov is fitted to take his place with Turgenev. Chekhov is preëminently the master of short stories. Within the limits of a few pages he paints the drama of human life with its manifold tragic and comic colors, in its most intimate reflex upon the characters who pass through the panorama. He has been called a pessimist. As if one could miss the sun without feeling the torture of utter darkness!

Chekhov wrote during the gloomiest period of Russian life, at a time when the reaction had drowned the revolution in the blood of the young generation,—when the Tsar had choked the very breath out of young Russia. The intellectuals were deprived of every outlet: all the social channels were closed to them, and they found themselves without hope or faith, not having yet learned to make common cause with the people.

Chekhov could not escape the atmosphere which darkened the horizon of almost the whole of Russia. It was because he so intensely felt its oppressive weight that he longed for air, for light, for new and vital ideas. To awaken the same yearning and faith in others, he had to picture life as it was, in all its wretchedness and horror.

This he did in "The Seagull," while in "The Cherry Orchard" he holds out the hope of a new and brighter day.

THE SEAGULL

In "The Seagull" the young artist, *Constantine Treplef*, seeks new forms, new modes of expression. He is tired of the old academic ways, the beaten track; he is disgusted with the endless imitative methods, no one apparently capable of an original thought.

Constantine has written a play; the principal part is to be acted by *Nina*, a beautiful girl with whom *Constantine* is in love. He arranges the first performance to take place on the occasion of his mother's vacation in the country.

She herself—known as *Mme. Arcadina*—is a famous actress of the old school. She knows how to show off her charms to advantage, to parade her beautiful gowns, to faint and die gracefully before the footlights; but she does not know how to live her part on the stage. *Mme. Arcadina* is the type of artist who lacks all conception of the relation between art and life. Barren of vision and empty of heart, her only criterion is public approval and material success. Needless to say, she cannot understand her son. She considers him decadent, a foolish rebel who wants to undermine the settled canons of dramatic art. *Constantine* sums up his mother's personality in the following manner:

Treplef. She is a psychological curiosity, is my mother. A clever and gifted woman, who can cry over a novel, will reel you off all Nekrassov's poems by heart, and is the perfection of a sick nurse; but venture to praise Eleonora Duse before her! Oho! ho! You must praise nobody but her, write about her, shout about her, and go into ecstasies over her wonderful performance in *La Dame aux Camélias*, or *The Fumes of Life;* but as she cannot have these intoxicating pleasures down here in the country, she's bored and gets spiteful. . . . She loves the stage; she thinks that she is advancing the cause of humanity and her sacred art; but I regard the stage of to-day as mere routine and prejudice. When the curtain goes up and the gifted beings, the high priests of the sacred art, appear by electric light, in a room with three sides to it, representing how people eat, drink, love, walk and wear their jackets; when they strive to squeeze out a moral from the flat, vulgar pictures and the flat, vulgar phrases, a little tiny moral, easy to comprehend and handy for home consumption, when in a thousand variations they offer me always the same thing over and over and over again—then I take to my heels and run, as Maupassant ran from the Eiffel Tower, which crushed his brain by its overwhelming vulgarity. . . . We must have new formulae. That's what we want. And if there are none, then it's better to have nothing at all.

With *Mme. Arcadina* is her lover, *Trigorin,* a successful writer. When he began his literary career, he possessed originality and strength. But gradually writing became a habit: the publishers constantly demand new books, and he supplies them.

Oh, the slavery of being an "arrived" artist, forging new chains for oneself with every "best seller"! Such is the position of *Trigorin:* he hates his work as the worst drudgery. Exhausted of ideas, all life and human relations serve him only as material for copy.

Nina, innocent of the ways of the world and saturated with the false romanticism of *Trigorin's* works, does not see the man but the celebrated artist. She is carried away by his fame and stirred by his presence; an infatuation with him quickly replaces her affection for *Constantine.* To her *Trigorin* embodies her dream of a brilliant and interesting life.

Nina. How I envy you, if you but knew it! How different are the lots of different people! Some can hardly drag on their tedious, insignificant existence; they are all alike, all miserable; others, like you, for instance—you are one in a million—are blessed with a brilliant, interesting life, all full of meaning. . . . You are happy. . . . What a delightful life yours is!

Trigorin. What is there so fine about it? Day and night I am obsessed by the same persistent thought; I must write, I must write, I must write. . . . No sooner have I finished one story than I am somehow compelled to write another, then a third, and after the third a fourth. . . . I have no rest for myself; I feel that I am devouring my own life. . . . I've never satisfied *myself.* . . . I have the feeling for nature; it wakes a passion in me, an irresistible desire to write. But I am something more than a landscape painter; I'm a citizen as well; I love my country, I love the people; I feel that if I am a writer I am bound to speak of the people, of its suffering, of its future, to speak of science, of the rights of man, etc., etc.; and I speak about it all, volubly, and am attacked angrily in return by everyone; I dart from side to side like a fox run down by hounds; I see that life and science fly farther and farther ahead of me, and I fall farther and farther behind, like the countryman running after the train; and in the end I feel that the only thing I can write of is the landscape, and in everything else I am untrue to life, false to the very marrow of my bones.

Constantine realizes that *Nina* is slipping away from him. The situation is aggravated by the constant friction with his mother and his despair at the lack of encouragement for his art. In a fit of despondency he attempts suicide, but without success. His mother, although nursing him back to health, is infuriated at her son's "foolishness," his inability to adapt himself to conditions, his impractical ideas. She decides to leave, accompanied by *Trigorin.* On the day of their departure *Nina* and *Trigorin* meet once more. The girl tells him of her ambition to become an actress, and, encouraged by him, follows him to the city.

Two years later *Mme. Arcadina,* still full of her idle triumphs, returns to her estate. *Trigorin* is again with her still haunted by the need of copy.

Constantine has in the interim matured considerably. Although he has made himself heard as a writer, he nevertheless feels that life to-day has no place for such as he: that sincerity in art is not wanted. His mother is with him, but she only serves to emphasize the flatness of his surroundings. He loves her, but her ways jar him and drive him into seclusion.

Nina, too, has returned to her native place, broken in body and spirit. Partly because of the memory of her past affection for *Constantine,* and mainly because she learns of *Trigorin's* presence, she is drawn to the place where two years before she had dreamed of the beauty of an artistic career. The cruel struggle for recognition, the bitter disappointment in her relation with *Trigorin,* the care of a child and poor health have combined to change the romantic child into a sad woman.

Constantine still loves her. He pleads with her to go away with him, to begin a new life. But it is too late. The lure of the footlights is beckoning to *Nina;* she returns to the stage. *Constantine,* unable to stand the loneliness of his life and the mercenary demands upon his art, kills himself.

To the Anglo-Saxon mind such an ending is pessimism,—defeat. Often, however, apparent defeat is in reality the truest success. For is not success, as commonly understood, but too frequently bought at the expense of character and idealism?

"The Seagull" is not defeat. As long as there is still such material in society as the Constantines—men and women who would rather die than compromise with the sordidness of life—there is hope for humanity. If the Constantines perish, it is the social fault,—our indifference to, and lack of appreciation of, the real values that alone advance the fuller and more complete life of the race.

THE CHERRY ORCHARD

"The Cherry Orchard" is Chekhov's prophetic song. In this play he depicts three stages of social development and their reflex in literature.

Mme. Ranevsky, the owner of the cherry orchard, an estate celebrated far and wide for its beauty and historic traditions, is deeply attached to the family place. She loves it for its romanticism: nightingales sing in the orchard, accompanying the wooing of lovers. She is devoted to it because of the memory of her ancestors and because of the many tender ties which bind her to the orchard. The same feeling and reverence is entertained by her brother

Leonid Gayef. They are expressed in the *Ode to an Old Family Cupboard:*

Gayef. Beloved and venerable cupboard; honor and glory to your existence, which for more than a hundred years has been directed to the noble ideals of justice and virtue. Your silent summons to profitable labor has never weakened in all these hundred years. You have upheld the courage of succeeding generations of human kind; you have upheld faith in a better future and cherished in us ideals of goodness and social consciousness.

But the social consciousness of *Gayef* and of his sister is of a paternal nature: the attitude of the aristocracy toward its serfs. It is a paternalism that takes no account of the freedom and happiness of the people,—the romanticism of a dying class.

Mme. Ranevsky is impoverished. The cherry orchard is heavily mortgaged and as romance and sentiment cannot liquidate debts, the beautiful estate falls into the cruel hands of commercialism.

The merchant *Yermolai Lopakhin* buys the place. He is in ecstasy over his newly acquired possession. He the owner—he who had risen from the serfs of the former master of the orchard!

Lopakhin. Just think of it! The cherry orchard is mine! Mine! Tell me that I'm drunk; tell me that I'm off my head; tell me that it's all a dream! . . . If only my father and my grandfather could rise from their graves and see the whole affair, how their Yermolai, their flogged and ignorant Yermolai, who used to run about barefooted in the winter, how this same Yermolai had bought a property that hasn't its equal for beauty anywhere in the whole world! I have bought the property where my father and grandfather were slaves, where they weren't even allowed into the kitchen.

A new epoch begins in the cherry orchard. On the ruins of romanticism and aristocratic ease there rises commercialism, its iron hand yoking nature, devastating her beauty, and robbing her of all radiance.

With the greed of rich returns, *Lopakhin* cries, "Lay the ax to the cherry orchard, come and see the trees fall down! We'll fill the place with villas."

Materialism reigns supreme; it lords the orchard with mighty hand, and in the frenzy of its triumph believes itself in control of the bodies and souls of men. But in the madness of conquest it has discounted a stubborn obstacle—the spirit of idealism. It is symbolized in *Peter Trophimof,* "the perpetual student," and *Anya,* the young daughter of *Mme. Ranevsky.* The "wonderful achievements" of the materialistic age do not enthuse them; they have emancipated themselves from the Lopakhin idol as well as from their aristocratic traditions.

Anya. Why is it that I no longer love the cherry orchard as I did? I used to love it so tenderly; I thought there was no better place on earth than our garden.

Trophimof. All Russia is our garden. The earth is great and beautiful; it is full of wonderful places. Think, Anya, your grandfather, your great-grandfather and all your ancestors were serf-owners, owners of living souls. Do not human spirits look out at you from every tree in the orchard, from every leaf and every stem? Do you not hear human voices? . . . Oh! it is terrible. Your orchard frightens me. When I walk through it in the evening or at night, the rugged bark on the trees glows with a dim light, and the cherry trees seem to see all that happened a hundred and two hundred years ago in painful and oppressive dreams. Well, well, we have fallen at least two hundred years beyond the times. We have achieved nothing at all as yet; we have not made up our minds how we stand with the past; we only philosophize, complain of boredom, or drink vodka. It is so plain that, before we can live in the present, we must first redeem the past, and have done with it.

Anya. The house we live in has long since ceased to be our house; I shall go away.

Trophimof. If you have the household keys, throw them in the well and go away. Be free, be free as the wind. . . . I am hungry as the winter; I am sick, anxious, poor as a beggar. Fate has tossed me hither and thither; I have been everywhere, everywhere. But everywhere I have been, every minute, day and night, my soul has been full of mysterious anticipations. I feel the approach of happiness, Anya; I see it coming . . . it is coming towards us, nearer and nearer; I can hear the sound of its footsteps. . . . And if we do not see it, if we do not know it, what does it matter? Others will see it.

The new generation, on the threshold of the new epoch, hears the approaching footsteps of the Future. And even if the Anyas and Trophimofs of to-day will not see it, others will.

It was not given to Anton Chekhov to see it with his bodily eyes. But his prophetic vision beheld the coming of the New Day, and with powerful pen he proclaimed it, that others might see it. Far from being a pessimist, as charged by unintelligent critics, his faith was strong in the possibilities of liberty.

This is the inspiring message of "The Cherry Orchard."

MAXIM GORKY

THE LOWER DEPTHS

We in America are conversant with tramp literature. A number of writers of considerable note have described what is commonly called the underworld, among them Josiah Flynt and Jack London, who have ably interpreted the life and psychology of the outcast. But with all due respect for their ability, it must be said that, after all, they wrote only as onlookers, as observers. They were not tramps themselves, in the real sense of the word. In "The Children of the Abyss" Jack London relates that when he stood in the breadline, he had money, a room in a good hotel, and a change of linen at hand. He was therefore not an integral part of the underworld, of the homeless and hopeless.

Never before has anyone given such a true, realistic picture of the social depths as Maxim Gorky, himself a denizen of the underworld from his early childhood. At the age of eight he ran away from his poverty-stricken, dismal home, and for many years thereafter he lived the life of the *bosyaki*. He tramped through the length and breadth of Russia; he lived with the peasant, the factory worker and the outcast. He knew them intimately; he understood their psychology, for he was not only with them, but of them. Therefore Gorky has been able to present such a vivid picture of the underworld.

"The Lower Depths" portrays a lodging house, hideous and foul, where gather the social derelicts,—the thief, the gambler, the ex-artist, the ex-aristocrat, the prostitute. All of them had at one time an ambition, a goal, but because of their lack of will and the injustice and cruelty of the world, they were forced into the depths and cast back whenever they attempted to rise. They are the superfluous ones, dehumanized and brutalized.

In this poisonous air, where everything withers and dies, we nevertheless find character. *Natasha,* a young girl, still retains her wholesome instincts. She had never known love or sympathy, had gone hungry all her days, and had tasted nothing but abuse from her brutal sister, on whom she was dependent. *Vaska Pepel,* the young thief, a lodger in the house, strikes a responsive chord in her the moment he makes her feel that he cares for her and that she might be of spiritual and moral help to him. *Vaska,* like *Natasha,* is a product of his social environment.

Vaska. From childhood, I have been—only a thief. . . . Always I was called Vaska the pickpocket, Vaska the son of a thief! See, it was of no consequence to me, as long as they would have it so . . . so they would have it. . . . I was a thief, perhaps, only out of spite . . . because nobody came along to call me anything—thief. . . . You call me something else, Natasha. . . . It is no easy life that I lead—friendless; pursued like a wolf. . . . I sink like a man in a swamp . . . whatever I touch is slimy and rotten . . . nothing is firm . . . but you are like a young fir-tree; you are prickly, but you give support.

There is another humane figure illuminating the dark picture in "The Lower Depths",—*Luka.* He is the type of an old pilgrim, a man whom the experiences of life have taught wisdom. He has tramped trough Russia and Siberia, and consorted with all sorts of people; but disappointment and grief have not robbed him of his faith in beauty, in idealism. He believes that every man, however low, degraded, or demoralized can yet be reached, if we but know how to touch his soul. *Luka* inspires courage and hope in everyone he meets, urging each to begin life anew. To the former actor, now steeped in drink, he says:

Luka. The drunkard, I have heard, can now be cured, without charge. They realize now, you see, that the drunkard is also a man. You must begin to make ready. Begin a new life!

Luka tries also to imbue *Natasha* and *Vaska* with new faith. They marvel at his goodness. In simplicity of heart *Luka* gives his philosophy of life.

Luka. I am good, you say. But you see, there must be some one to be good. . . . We must have pity on mankind. . . . Have pity while there is still time, believe me, it is very good. I was once, for example, employed as a watchman, at a country place which belonged to an engineer, not far from the city of Tomsk, in Siberia. The house stood in the middle of the forest, an out-of-the-way location . . . and it was winter and I was all alone in the country house. It was beautiful there . . . magnificent! And once . . . I heard them scrambling up! . . .

Natasha. Thieves!

Luka. Yes. They crept higher and I took my rifle and went outside. I looked up: two men . . . as they were opening a window and so busy that they did not see anything of me at all. I cried to them: "Heh there . . . get out of that" . . . and would you think it, they fell on me with a hand ax. . . . I warned them—"Halt," I cried, "or else I fire" . . . then I aimed first at one and then at the other. They fell on their knees, saying, "Pardon us." I was pretty hot . . . on account of the hand ax, you remember. "You devils," I cried, "I told you to clear out and you didn't . . . and now," I said, "one of you go into the brush and get a switch." It was done. "And now," I commanded, "one of you stretch out on the ground, and the other thrash him" . . . and so they whipped each other at my command. And when they had each had a sound beating, they said to me: "Grandfather," said they, "for the sake of Christ give us a piece of bread. We haven't a bite in our bodies." They were the thieves, who had fallen upon me with the hand ax. Yes . . . they were a pair of splendid fellows. . . . I said to them, "If you had asked for bread." Then they answered: "We had gotten past that. . . . We had asked and asked and nobody would give us anything . . . endurance was worn out," . . . and so they remained with me the whole winter. One of them, Stephen by name, liked to take the rifle and go into the woods . . . and the other, Jakoff, was constantly ill, always coughing . . . the three of us watched the place, and when spring came, they said, "Farewell, grandfather," and went away—to Russia. . . .

Natasha. Were they convicts, escaping?

Luka. They were . . . fugitives . . . they had left their colony . . . a pair of splendid fellows. . . . If I had not had pity on them—who knows what would have happened. They might have killed me. . . . Then they would be taken to court again, put in prison, sent back to Siberia. . . . Why all that? You learn nothing good in prison, nor in Siberia . . . but a man, what can he not learn. Man may teach his fellowman something good . . . very simply.

Impressed and strengthened by *Luka's* wonderful faith and vision, the unfortunates make an attempt to rise from the social swamp. But he has come too late into their lives. They have been robbed of energy and will; and conditions always conspire to thrust them back into the depths. When *Natasha* and *Vaska* are about to start out on the road to a new life, fate overtakes them. The girl, during a scene with her heartless sister, is terribly scalded by the latter, and *Vaska,* rushing to the defense of his sweetheart, encounters her brutal brother-in-law, whom he accidentally kills. Thus these "superfluous ones" go down in the struggle. Not because of their vicious or degrading tendencies; on the contrary, it is their better instincts that cause them to be swept back into the abyss. But though they perish, the inspiration of *Luka* is not entirely lost. It is epitomized in the words of one of the victims.

Sahtin. The old man—he lived from within. . . . He saw everything with his own eyes. . . . I asked him once: "Grandfather, why do men really live?"

... "Man lives ever to give birth to strength. There live, for example, the carpenters, noisy, miserable people . . . and suddenly in their midst is a carpenter born . . . such a carpenter as the world has never seen: he is above all, no other carpenter can be compared to him. He gives a new face to the whole trade . . . his own face, so to speak . . . and with that simple impulse it has advanced twenty years . . . and so the others live . . . the locksmiths and the shoemakers, and all the rest of the working people . . . and the same is true of other classes—all to give birth to strength. Everyone thinks that he for himself takes up room in the world, but it turns out that he is here for another's benefit—for someone better . . . a hundred years . . . or perhaps longer . . . if we live so long . . . for the sake of genius. . . . All, my children, all, live only to give birth to strength. For that reason we must respect everybody. We cannot know who he is, for what purpose born, or what he may yet fulfill . . . perhaps he has been born for our good fortune . . . or great benefit."

No stronger indictment than "The Lower Depths" is to be found in contemporary literature of our perverse civilization that condemns thousands—often the very best men and women—to the fate of the Vaskas and Anyas, doomed as superfluous and unnecessary in society. And yet they are necessary, aye, they are vital, could we but see beneath the veil of cold indifference and stupidity to discover the deep humanity, the latent possibilities in these lowliest of the low. If within our social conditions they are useless material, often vicious and detrimental to the general good, it is because they have been denied opportunity and forced into conditions that kill their faith in themselves and all that is best in their natures.

The so-called depravity and crimes of these derelicts are fundamentally the depravity and criminal anti-social attitude of Society itself that first creates the underworld and, having created it, wastes much energy and effort in suppressing and destroying the menacing phantom of its own making,—forgetful of the elemental brotherhood of man, blind to the value of the individual, and ignorant of the beautiful possibilities inherent in even the most despised children of the depths.

LEONID ANDREYEV

KING HUNGER

LEONID ANDREYEV is the youngest and at the present time the most powerful dramatist of Russia. Like Chekhov and Gorky, he is very versatile: his sketches and stories possess as fine a literary quality and stirring social appeal as his plays.

No one who has read his terrible picture of war, "The Red Laugh," or his unsurpassed arraignment of capital punishment, "The Seven Who Were Hanged," can erase from memory the effect of Leonid Andreyev's forceful pen.

The drama "King Hunger" deals with the most powerful king on earth,—*King Hunger*. In the presence of *Time* and *Death* he pleads with *Time* to ring the alarm, to call the people to rebellion, because the earth is replete with suffering: cities, shops, mines, factories and fields resound with the moans and groans of the people. Their agony is unbearable.

King Hunger. Strike the bell, old man; rend to the ears its copper mouth. Let no one slumber!

But *Time* has no faith in *King Hunger*. He knows that *Hunger* had deceived the people on many occasions: "You will deceive again, King Hunger. You have many a time deluded your children and me." Yet *Time* is weary with waiting. He consents to strike the bell.

King Hunger calls upon the workingmen to rebel. The scene is in a machine shop; the place is filled with deafening noises as of men's groans. Every machine, every tool, every screw, holds its human forms fettered to it and all keep pace with the maddening speed of their tormentors. And through the thunder and clatter of iron there rises the terrible plaint of the toilers.

——We are starving.

——We are crushed by machines.

——Their weight smothers us.

——The iron crushes.

——The steel oppresses.

——Oh, what a furious weight! As a mountain upon me!

——The whole earth is upon me.

——The iron hammer flattens me. It crushes the blood out of my veins, it fractures my bones, it makes me flat as sheet iron.

——Through the rollers my body is pressed and drawn thin as wire. Where is my body? Where is my blood? Where is my soul?

——The wheel is twirling me.

——Day and night screaks the saw cutting steel. Day and night in my ears the screeching of the saw cutting steel. All the dreams that I see, all the sounds and songs that I hear, is the screeching of the saw cutting steel. What is the earth? It is the screeching of the saw. What is the sky? It is the screeching of the saw cutting steel. Day and night.

——Day and night.

——We are crushed by the machines.

——We ourselves are parts of the machines.

——Brothers! We forge our own chains!

The crushed call upon *King Hunger* to help them, to save them from the horror of their life. Is he not the most powerful king on earth?

King Hunger comes and exhorts them to rebel. All follow his call except three. One of these is huge of body, of Herculean build, large of muscle but with small, flat head upon his massive shoulders. The second workingman is young, but with the mark of death already upon his brow. He is constantly coughing and the hectic flush on his cheeks betrays the wasting disease of his class. The third workingman is a worn-out old man. Everything about him, even his voice, is deathlike, colorless, as if in his person a thousand lives had been robbed of their bloom.

First Workingman. I am as old as the earth. I have performed all the twelve labors, cleansed stables, cut off the hydra's heads, dug and vexed the earth, built cities, and have so altered its face, that the Creator himself would not readily recognize her. But I can't say why I did all this. Whose will did I shape? To what end did I aspire? My head is dull. I am dead tired. My strength oppresses me. Explain it to me, O King! Or I'll clutch this hammer and crack the earth as a hollow nut.

King Hunger. Patience, my son! Save your powers for the last great revolt. Then you'll know all.

First Workingman. I shall wait.

Second Workingman. He cannot comprehend it, O King. He thinks that we must crack the earth. It is a gross falsehood, O King! The earth is fair as the garden of God. We must guard and caress her as a little girl. Many that stand there in the darkness say, there is no sky, no sun, as if eternal night is upon the earth. Just think: eternal night!

King Hunger. Why, coughing blood, do you smile and gaze to heaven?

Second Workingman. Because flowers will blossom on my blood, and I see them now. On the breast of a beautiful rich lady I saw a red rose—she didn't know it was my blood.

King Hunger. You are a poet, my son. I suppose you write verses, as they do.

Second Workingman. King, O King, sneer not at me. In darkness I learned to worship fire. Dying I understood that life is enchanting. Oh, how enchanting! King, it shall become a great garden, and there shall walk in peace, unmolested, men and animals. Dare not ruffle the animals! Wrong not any man! Let them play, embrace, caress one another—let them! But where is the path? Where is the path? Explain, King Hunger.

King Hunger. Revolt.

Second Workingman. Through violence to freedom? Through blood to love and kisses?

King Hunger. There is no other way.

Third Workingman. You lie, King Hunger. Then you have killed my father and grandfather and great-grandfather, and would'st thou kill us? Where do you lead us, unarmed? Don't you see how ignorant we are, how blind and impotent. You are a traitor. Only here you are a king, but there you lackey upon their tables. Only here you wear a crown, but there you walk about with a napkin.

King Hunger will not listen to their protest. He gives them the alternative of rebellion or starvation for themselves and their children. They decide to rebel, for *King Hunger* is the most powerful king on earth.

The subjects of *King Hunger,* the people of the underworld, gather to devise ways and means of rebellion. A gruesome assembly this, held in the cellar. Above is the palace ringing with music and laughter, the fine ladies in gorgeous splendor, bedecked with flowers and costly jewels, the tables laden with rich food and delicious wines. Everything is most exquisite there, joyous and happy. And underneath in the cellar, the underworld is gathered, all the dregs of society: the robber and the murderer, the thief and the prostitute, the gambler and the drunkard. They have come to consult with each other how poverty is to rebel, how to throw off the yoke, and what to do with the rich.

Various suggestions are made. One advises poisoning the supply of water. But this is condemned on the ground that the people also have to drink from the same source.

Another suggests that all books should be burned for they teach the rich how to oppress. But the motion fails. What is the use of burning the books? The wealthy have money; they will buy writers, poets and scientists to make new books.

A third proposes that the children of the rich be killed. From the darkest, most dismal corner of the cellar comes the protest of an old woman: "Oh, not the children. Don't touch the children. I have buried many of them myself. I know the pain of the mother. Besides, the children are not to blame for the crimes of their parents. Don't touch the children! The child is pure and sacred. Don't hurt the child!"

A little girl rises, a child of twelve with the face of the aged. She announces that for the last four years she has given her body for money. She had been sold by her mother because they needed bread for the smaller children. During the four years of her terrible life, she has consorted with all kinds of men, influential men, rich men, pious men. They infected her. Therefore she proposes that the rich should be infected.

The underworld plans and plots, and the gruesome meeting is closed with a frenzied dance between *King Hunger* and *Death,* to the music of the dance above.

King Hunger is at the trial of the *Starving.* He is the most powerful king on earth: he is at home everywhere, but nowhere more so than at the trial of the *Starving.* On high chairs sit the judges, in all their bloated importance. The courtroom is filled with curiosity seekers, idle ladies dressed as if for a ball; college professors and students looking for object lessons in criminal depravity; rich young girls are there, to satisfy a perverted craving for excitement.

The first starveling is brought in muzzled.

King Hunger. What is your offense, starveling?
Old Man. I stole a five-pound loaf, but it was wrested from me. I had only time to bite a small piece of it. Forgive me, I will never again—

He is condemned in the name of the *Law* and *King Hunger,* the most powerful king on earth.

Another starveling is brought before the bar of justice. It is a woman, young and beautiful, but pale and sad. She is charged with killing her child.

Young Woman. One night my baby and I crossed the long bridge over the river. And since I had long before decided, so then approaching the middle, where the river is deep and swift, I said: "Look, baby dear, how the water is a-roaring below." She said, "I can't reach, mamma, the railing is so high." I said, "Come, let me lift you, baby dear." And when she was gazing down into the black deep, I threw her over. That's all.

The *Law* and *King Hunger* condemn the woman to "blackest hell," there to be "tormented and burned in everlasting, slackless fires."

The heavy responsibility of meting out justice has fatigued the judges. The excitement of the trial has sharpened the appetite of the spectators. *King Hunger,* at home with all people, proposes that the court adjourn for luncheon.

The scene in the restaurant represents Hunger devouring like a wild beast the produce of toil, ravenous, famished, the victim of his own gluttonous greed.

The monster fed, his hunger and thirst appeased, he now returns to sit in self-satisfied judgment over the *Starving.* The judges are more bloated than before, the ladies more eager to bask in the misery of their fellows. The college professors and students, mentally heavy with food, are still anxious to add data to the study of human criminality.

A lean boy is brought in, muzzled; he is followed by a ragged woman.

Woman. Have mercy! He stole an apple for me, your Honor. I was sick, thought he. "Let me bring her a little apple." Pity him! Tell them that you won't any more. Well! Speak!

Starveling. I won't any more.

Woman. I've already punished him myself. Pity his youth, cut not at the root his bright little days!

Voices. Indeed, pity one and then the next. cut the evil at its roots.

——One needs courage to be ruthless.

——It is better for them.

——Now he is only a boy, but when he grows up——

King Hunger. Starveling, you are condemned.

A starveling, heavily muzzled, is dragged in. He is big and strong. He protests to the court: he has always been a faithful slave. But *King Hunger* announces that the man is dangerous, because the faithful slave, being strong and honest, is "obnoxious to people of refined culture and less brawny." The slave is faithful to-day, *King Hunger* warns the judges, but "who can trust the to-morrow? Then in his strength and integrity we will encounter a violent and dangerous enemy."

In the name of justice the faithful slave is condemned. Finally the last starveling appears. He looks half human, half beast.

King Hunger. Who are you, starveling? Answer. Do you understand human speech?

Starveling. We are the peasants.

King Hunger. What's your offense?

Starveling. We killed the devil.

King Hunger. It was a man whom you burnt.

Starveling. No, it was the devil. The priest told us so, and then we burnt him.

The peasant is condemned. The session of the Court closes with a brief speech by *King Hunger.*

King Hunger. To-day you witnessed a highly instructive spectacle. Divine, eternal justice has found in us, as judges and your retainers, its brilliant reflection on earth. Subject only to the laws of immortal equity, unknown to culpable compassion, indifferent to cursing and entreating prayers, obeying the voice of our conscience alone—we illumed this earth with the light of human wisdom and sublime, sacred truth. Not for a single moment forgetting that justice is the foundation of life, we have crucified the Christ in days gone by and since, to this very day, we cease not to grace Golgotha with new crosses. But, certainly, only ruffians, only ruffians are hanged. We showed no mercy to God himself, in the name of the laws of immortal justice—would we be now disconcerted by the howling of this impotent, starving rabble, by their cursing and raging? Let them curse! Life herself blesses us, the great sacred truth will screen us with her veil, and the very decree of history will not be more just than our own. What have they gained by cursing? What? They are there, we're here. They are in dungeons, in galleys, on crosses, but we will go to the theater. They perish, but we will devour them—devour—devour.

The court has fulfilled its mission. *King Hunger* is the most powerful king on earth.

The starvelings break out in revolt. The bells peal with deafening thunder; all is confusion and chaos. The city is immersed in the blackness of despair, and all is dark. Now and then gusts of fire sweep the sky illuminating the scene of battle. The air is filled with cries and groans; there is the thud of falling bodies, and still the fight goes on.

In a secluded part of the town stands the castle. In its most magnificent ballroom the rich and their lackeys—scientists, teachers and artists—are gathered. They tremble with fear at the ominous sounds outside. To silence the loud beat of their terror they command the musicians to strike up the liveliest tunes, and the guests whirl about in a mad dance.

From time to time the door is forced open and someone drops exhausted to the floor. An artist rushes in, crying out that the art gallery is in flames.

"Murillo is burning! Velasquez is burning! Giorgione is burning!"

He is not in the least concerned with living values; he dwells in the past and he wildly bewails the dead weight of the past.

One after another men rush in to report the burning of libraries, the breaking of statues, and the destruction of monuments. No one among the wealthy mob regrets the slaughter of human life.

Panic-stricken the mighty fall from their thrones. The Starving, infuriated and vengeful, are marching on the masters! They must not see the craven fear of the huddled figures in the mansions,—the lights are turned off. But darkness is even more terrible to the frightened palace mob. In the madness of terror they begin to accuse and denounce each other. They feel as helpless as children before the approaching avalanche of vengeance.

At this critical moment a man appears. He is small, dirty, and unwashed; he smells of cheap whisky and bad tobacco; he blows his nose with a red handkerchief and his manners are disgusting. He is the engineer. He looks calmly about him, presses a button, and the place is flooded with light. He brings the comforting news that the revolt is crushed.

Engineer. On Sunny Hill we planted a line of immense machine guns of enormous power. . . . A few projectiles of a specially destructive power. . . . A public square filled with people . . . Enough one or two such shells. . . . And should the revolt still continue, we'll shower the city.

The revolt is over. All is quiet—the peace of death. The ground is strewn with bodies, the streets are soaked with blood. Fine ladies flit about. They lift their children and bid them kiss the mouth of the cannon, for the cannon have saved the rich from destruction. Prayers and hymns are offered up to the cannon, for they have saved the masters and punished the starvelings. And all is quiet, with the stillness of the graveyard where sleep the dead.

King Hunger, with hollow cheeks and sunken eyes, makes a desperate last appeal to his children.

King Hunger. Oh, my son, my son! You clamored so loud—why are you mute? Oh, my daughter, my daughter, you hated so profoundly, so intensely, you most miserable on earth—arise. Arise from the dust! Rend the shadowy bonds of death! Arise! I conjure you in the name of Life!— You're silent?

For a brief moment all remains silent and immovable. Suddenly a sound is heard, distant at first, then nearer and nearer, till a thousand-throated roar breaks forth like thunder:

——We shall yet come!
——We shall yet come!
——Woe unto the victorious!

The Victors pale at the ghostly cry. Seized with terror, they run, wildly howling:

——The dead arise!
——The dead arise!

"We shall yet come!" cry the dead. For they who died for an ideal never die in vain. They must come back, they shall come back. And then—woe be to the victorious! *King Hunger* is indeed the most terrible king on earth, but only for those who are driven by blind forces alone.

But they who can turn on the light, know the power of the things they have created. They will come, and take possession,—no longer the wretched scum, but the masters of the world.

A message revolutionary, deeply social in its scope, illumining with glorious hope the dismal horizon of the disinherited of the earth.